IT MUST BE
A
Big
Game

50 YEARS OF COVERING SPORTS

IT MUST BE
A
Big
Game

50 YEARS OF COVERING SPORTS

Al Pickett

Cover photo: Shayli Anne Photography

Photo on page 232: Loretta Fulton

Other photos are from the author's personal collection.

© 2025, Al Pickett

ISBN: 979-8-9988655-1-0

Published by Texas Star Trading Company
174 Cypress Street, Abilene, Texas 79601
www.TexasStarTrading.com
(325) 672-9696

Design by Lauren Monsey, Monsey Creative LLC

Printed in the USA

Dedicated to my family
Carole, Jay, Christy, Jaxon, Ashton,
Troy, Kristy, Landen, Katelynn,
Cagan, Kenzi

Table of Contents

Foreword

Al Pickett is one of the best sportswriters I've had the pleasure of knowing.

Al is a terrific storyteller, columnist, author, broadcaster, creator of a regional sports hall of fame, family man, and church and civic leader – respected statewide, and especially in his hometown.

In many ways, he's the sportswriter I wanted to be – before my career path took me in different directions. When I was a newspaper editor, one of the best things I did for the newspaper and the city was to recruit Al Pickett to move from Arkansas to Abilene and be our sports editor. Later, as a book publisher, I asked Al to write a book that became a perennial local best-seller on the Abilene High *Team of the Century* football dynasty under Chuck Moser. He would go on to write *The Greatest Texas Sports Stories You've Never Heard* (my favorite, still in print), *Brother's Keeper* (made into a movie) and books about legendary coaches Emory Bellard and Jimmie Keeling.

What a difference Al has made in Abilene and in Texas as a sports editor, radio talk show host, college and high school play-by-play announcer, freelance journalist, and chairman of the Big Country Athletic Hall of Fame.

And what great stories he can tell about his fifty years covering sports. Sit back and enjoy what he has to say.

Glenn Dromgoole
Abilene, Texas

Introduction

I feel blessed to have been able to make a living covering sports for fifty years. My career has been unusual in that I have been both a play-by-play announcer on the radio for more than thirty years and a newspaper sports editor for nineteen years. During that time, I have also written for other newspapers and magazines as a freelance writer and hosted a radio sports talk show for nearly twenty years.

I also feel blessed that my career covered what I call the end of the glory years for both forms of media. The hours were long and the pay was little, but I think we had more fun than those in the business today.

My career actually dates back more than fifty years. I played basketball and ran track and cross country in high school, as well as played summer baseball, but I didn't play football. Not a lot of call for a skinny 135-pounder with no speed.

But somehow (I don't remember how) I got a job of writing the high school football game stories as a junior and senior for my hometown paper, the *Council Grove Republican*, which is still the smallest town in Kansas to have a daily newspaper. It was a fun experience as the Braves went 7-2 and 8-1 with two of the best teams in school history. My good friend and classmate Luis Hill was also the leading rusher in the state as a senior, which gave me plenty of good things to write about.

My career after college included eight years in radio in Marysville, Kansas, and Searcy, Arkansas, before becoming the sports editor of the *Searcy Daily Citizen*. I then moved to Abilene, Texas, to become the sports editor of the *Abilene Reporter-News* for fifteen years. For the past twenty-four years I have kept my hand in the sports world as host of a sports talk radio show, freelance writing for several magazines and newspapers, doing play-by-play announcing of local high school and college football, basketball and baseball games, and serving as chairman of the Big Country Athletic Hall of Fame.

The newspaper world has totally changed. With big corporations and hedge funds making decisions for the bottom line rather than what is best for the readers and the communities they serve, the newspaper has lost its importance. It has lost the franchise that it once held as the leading news source.

Sure, the internet now provides a myriad of other sources to get your sports fix. But there is no substitute for a community daily newspaper. The *Abilene Reporter-News* had the reputation of outstanding regional high school coverage. Readers eagerly awaited the arrival of their Saturday morning paper during football season to not only see the Friday night scores but to also read the box score of each game.

We would have complete statistics and scoring summaries of at least forty games every Saturday morning. Who had the big game rushing or passing? Who were the names to look for in your next opponent? What did the paper say about your favorite team's game? It was all there every Saturday morning.

The newspaper also provided a box score every Wednesday and Saturday morning for area boys and girls high school teams during basketball season, as well as baseball and softball line scores and tennis, golf and track results in the spring and volleyball and cross country results in the fall.

It may not necessarily be award-winning journalism all the time, but getting hundreds if not thousands of names in the paper each day sells newspapers. It is what readers want, a fact that is seemingly lost on today's newspaper management. To me, that is what a local – or regional – newspaper should be.

Now, readers can sometimes find some scores more quickly on the internet, but they don't get the statistics from a Sweetwater-Snyder game or a Stamford-Haskell matchup, for example. In fact, for the last year, one can't even find the results of games involving the local Abilene high school and college teams in the *Abilene Reporter-News* as well as the other smaller schools in the region. The same is true in Wichita Falls, Lubbock, Amarillo, San Angelo and many other papers around the state.

To me, a newspaper should be a publication of record of what is happening in its community or coverage area. My wife kept a scrapbook with game stories for our grandson in baseball and football and our granddaughter in volleyball. That is no longer possible for parents and grandparents.

It really doesn't matter if it is a printed newspaper or an online publication. Either way, most newspapers are no longer providing the coverage that they once did, mostly because they no longer have the manpower or because of edicts from out-of-market ownership that has no vested interest in the community they are supposed to serve.

The radio world has changed, too. Live streaming has allowed viewers to not only listen but to also watch some games. That is a good thing. But radio stations owned by conglomerates are no longer willing to broadcast as many games as they once did. For example, my first year working for locally owned KWKC/KSER in Searcy, Arkansas, I broadcast 101 basketball games that year. If it bounced, I probably called it.

As a "local" sportscaster/sportswriter, some might claim I didn't get to cover many "big" games. No World Series or Super Bowls or NCAA championships. Much of what I did was routine, making sure the high school and local college games stories were in the paper on deadline. But I feel like I was blessed to have covered "big" games nearly every week. They were big for those involved, and I tried to treat them that way. And I was privileged to cover ten Cotton Bowl games and numerous Dallas Cowboys, Texas Rangers, Southwest Conference and Big 12 football games during my career.

One of my sportswriters during my tenure at the *Abilene*

Reporter-News once complained to good friend Chuck Statler, who later became my broadcast partner for fifteen years on Abilene High football broadcasts, that I always assigned myself to cover the "big" games.

Actually, it was probably a fair complaint. I would rather be at a "big" game than sitting in the office.

Because of that, it became a running joke. Every time I would walk into the press box at Abilene's Shotwell Stadium, Chuck would say, "Al's here, it must be a big game." Still, to this day, when he calls me on the telephone, he will preface the call with "Hey, Big Game."

Thus, the title for this book. It is not meant to be a memoir but a collection of stories that I have accumulated over fifty years as a "local" sportscaster or sportswriter. My belief is sports are supposed to be fun and exciting. That is what I tried to bring to readers and listeners all those years.

I hope you will find these behind-the-scenes anecdotes and stories interesting, funny, entertaining and informative because if I was there, "It Must Be A Big Game."

Al Pickett

The Early Days

The majority of the stories in this book are experiences from my fifty-year-plus career of sports writing and broadcasting. But two of my favorite stories preceded that.

When I was in the eighth grade, my best friend Van Sammons' parents got tickets to Saturday night's games in the NCAA Midwest Regional tournament in 1967 at famed Allen Fieldhouse at the University of Kansas in Lawrence. It was just the second college basketball game I had seen in person.

That tournament featured a number of tremendous players – Wes Unseld of Louisville, Jo Jo White of Kansas and Elvin Hayes of Houston, to name a few – who went on to be stars in the National Basketball Association.

In those days, they played a third-place game. Louisville and Kansas were meeting in the third-place game, while Houston and Southwest Conference champion Southern Methodist University squared off for the regional championship and the right to go to the Final Four.

Our seats were up in the corner of Allen Fieldhouse and near the top of the section. In other words, our seats were about as far away from the court as they could be and still be in the arena.

At halftime of the third-place game, Van and I devised a plan to get closer to the court. Allen Fieldhouse, like many of the arenas of that era, had a dirt surface so it could be used for indoor track meets, too, after basketball season ended. The basketball court was a raised wooden floor. Coaches and players on the bench had to take a step up to get on the court.

Van and I went and sat under the basket, with our feet under the wooden court so that the court surface came to our chest. There was a walkway between the end of the court and the first row of the bleachers, so we weren't blocking anyone's view or people walking to their seats.

To our surprise, no one ran us off. We sat there, watching the second half of the third-place game and the entire championship game. We were sitting just ten or so feet away from the end line of the court. We watched Elvin Hayes score thirty-six points right in front of us as Houston whipped SMU to earn the first of three straight matchups with UCLA in the Final Four. We were mesmerized because it was the first time we had seen a big man who could score both inside and outside. He was amazing.

Years later, Van and I laughed, still wondering why no one ran us off the end of the court when we didn't have passes to be sitting there. I guess it was my first experience at wanting to be courtside for a "big game."

The other story involves coaching baseball. In the summer of 1974 between my junior and senior year of college, my last year living at home with my parents, I was working two jobs to pay for college and also played on a slow-pitch softball team.

My twelve-year-old next-door neighbor didn't have a coach for his Little League team, so his older brother and I agreed to coach the team. It was a fun experience, and we won the league championship.

The league involved ten-, eleven- and twelve-year-olds, and rules required every kid play in every game.

My favorite story involved Wes, one of the ten-year-old players on my team who was certainly not one of our better players. We were playing in the fifth inning of a tie game with the go-ahead runner on at second base and Wes at the plate.

I had taught the kids some very basic signs that I would deliver from the third-base coach's box. Wes got a count of three balls and no strikes, so I gave him the "take" sign, just hoping he would get a walk.

Wes, however, lined the next pitch into center field, driving in the runner from second with the winning run. Wes was the hero, and as the kids celebrated, I never said a word to him about missing the sign.

A couple of games later, it was the same situation: three balls and no strikes on Wes. I gave him the "take" sign again and he swung and missed. I never questioned players during the game, so at the next practice, I asked Wes why he swung at the pitch when he had a "take" sign.

"Coach, I thought the 'take' sign meant you had to take a swing," Wes replied.

I laughed. How could you argue with logic like that?

———

Years later, I coached my own boys in Little League, and I wrote a column about the funny things you see in youth baseball. I invited others to send in their favorite stories.

My favorite came from a father who was coaching his son on a T-ball team. A runner got on first base, and the coach told him that when the ball is hit, he was supposed to run straight to third base. "Don't stop until you get to third base."

The ball was hit, and the runner did exactly what the coach told him: He went directly to third base, running over the pitcher's mound and skipping second base all together.

"I learned I needed to be a little more explicit in my directions," the coach chuckled.

Column Writing

Big-city newspapers have writers who primarily write columns and nothing else. They are the personality of the newspaper.

I grew up reading Bob Hentzen of the Topeka Capitol-Journal. I later enjoyed reading Orville Henry of the Arkansas Gazette, Blackie Sherrod and Kevin Sherrington of the Dallas Morning News, and Kirk Bohls of the Austin American-Statesmen, just to name a few. It is the first thing I read when I pick up a newspaper.

When I made the transition from eight years of working in radio to become the sports editor of a one-man sports staff at the *Searcy (Arkansas) Daily Citizen*, I decided I wanted to write a column at least several days a week. I called it "Let's Talk Sports" in reference to my five years of working in radio in Searcy.

A column can mean a lot of different things. It has a picture of the columnist at the top of the article. It can be an opinion piece or a way to analyze a bigger issue. It could be something personal. It could be a notes column, an opportunity to include a number of items that didn't make the paper otherwise. Or it could be a sidebar to a game story in the same issue. By writing a column, I felt I could bring my personality to the sports page and make my sports section something different.

When I moved to the *Abilene Reporter-News* to head up a six-man sports staff at a regional newspaper in West Texas, I kept the same philosophy. I wrote several columns a week, and I encouraged our reporters to write columns, too. Our sports section in Abilene included weekly columns on our two local college conferences, a golf column, a bowling column, a hunting and fishing column, and even a recreation and competition tips column from Rick Meyers, a local former professional tennis player. None of those things exist today in the *Reporter-News*.

One of the columns that I am most proud of is one I wrote in March of 1983. The Searcy High School girls basketball team had just lost in the state basketball tournament semifinals with a team of all underclassmen. It seemed like the Lady Lions might have a chance to win a state championship the next year.

Unlike Texas, which holds its state tournament at the Alamodome in San Antonio each year, Arkansas at that time held its boys and girls state tournament in each classification at a different site. Cities bid on the right to host the state tournament.

The Searcy community and Harding University have a great relationship, but Harding had never hosted a state high school basketball tournament. Searcy High School's gym wasn't big enough to hold a state tournament (Searcy has since built a new gym), but Harding's Ganus Center could hold nearly 5,000 fans.

Without asking anyone, I wrote a column urging Searcy to bid to host the 1984 Class 3A boys and girls state tournament. There was risk in doing this, of course. What if the Lady Lions didn't qualify for the state tournament, and Searcy would hold a state tournament with no local interest?

To my delight, however, the two booster groups, the Searcy Lionbackers and the Harding Bison Booster Club, got together and secured the bid to host the state tournament. It couldn't have worked out better.

The Searcy girls lost just one game all season and rolled to the state championship in front of a capacity crowd of 5,000 appreciative hometown fans. What a thrill to see an idea come to fruition.

———

I estimate I have written more than 2,000 columns in 19 years as a newspaper sports editor. Above, I described the various different types of columns. One of my all-time favorite columns didn't really fit any of those categories, however, but it was a fascinating story.

The two state papers in Arkansas – the Gazette and the Democrat – carried the state's best high school track times during the spring each year. It is something we did in Abilene, too. Below the list of the top ten times, heights or distances in each event, the two Little Rock papers listed the state record in that event.

It was 1984, and the oldest record was twenty-four feet even in the boys long jump set by Win Whipple of Arkadelphia fifty years earlier in 1934. I covered a lot of high school track meets, and I often talked about that record with numerous coaches.

The normal comment was "Who in the heck was Win Whipple?" Or "What kind of tape measure did they have in 1934?" No one had ever heard of Win Whipple.

So I called my friend Rex Nelson, who is a senior columnist for the Arkansas Democrat-Gazette and is a champion of writing about all things Arkansas. Rex and I became friends when I was broadcasting Harding football and he was broadcasting Ouachita Baptist football, which happens to be his alma mater. Like me, he has had a career in both radio and newspapers. Unlike me, however, Rex also worked in politics for a time for then Arkansas Governor Mike Huckabee. He still does the Ouachita Baptist football play-by-play.

This was before the internet that allowed one to do research, but Rex grew up in Arkadelphia so I figured he might know the story of Win Whipple. The story he told me was absolutely fascinating.

Win Whipple was legitimate. He set the Arkansas state long jump record as a senior at Arkadelphia High School in 1934. He then went to LSU where he competed in 1935. He reportedly hitchhiked to the Drake Relays in Des Moines, Iowa, and the

Penn Relays in Philadelphia where he lost his only two events that spring to Jesse Owens.

Whipple was then diagnosed with sarcoma, cancer of the bone marrow. In 1936, when Owens was winning four gold medals in the Olympics in Berlin, Germany, Whipple was listening to the Olympics on the radio. He was in the hospital after having his leg amputated. He died in 1937.

I can't tell you how many coaches thanked me for that story, revealing the mystery of Win Whipple. My thanks to Rex Nelson, who provided me one of my favorite and most fascinating columns about the long-forgotten story of Win Whipple, whose remarkable career was cut way too short by cancer.

Remembering Scooter

Fans of College Game Day on ESPN in November 2024 mourned with noted college football analyst Kirk Herbstreit when he announced the death of his golden retriever Ben, who traveled everywhere with Herbstreit and often appeared on the set of College Game Day.

Ben became a star in his own right, drawing signs and attention at major college football games around the country. Condolences poured in for Ben. Everyone can relate to the loss of a dog that becomes such a part of our family's life.

I mentioned earlier that columns can be personal, and perhaps no column I ever wrote was more personal than the one I wrote for the *Abilene Reporter-News* on February 10, 1996. The headline read "Texas turned out to be a good fit for this old friend." Here is that column as reprinted from the *Reporter-News*:

Please grant the old sports editor a few personal notes today.

There are more than a few tears shed around the Pickett household this weekend.

We've lost a family member. Scooter, our family dog for

eleven years, died Friday, finally succumbing to cancer and old age.

While this may not be a sports story, Scooter became a sports personality in her own right when Weekend section editor Greg Jaklewicz ghost-wrote a story with her several years ago, describing how she was the brains behind my NFL picks.

She gave her predictions for the NFL playoffs that year and even wore a Houston Oilers cap in the picture (That was so long ago the Oilers were in the playoffs then and the Cowboys weren't.).

That is just one of many pictures we have of Scooter. It seems that almost every picture we have taken in our ten years in Abilene has somehow managed to include Scooter in it, whether it was playing in the back yard or unwrapping Christmas presents.

But this is the story of the best picture of Scooter that we failed to take.

Most families pick out their dogs. Just the opposite was true with Scooter. She picked us out.

It was about this time of year in 1985 when Scooter just showed up one day at our house. We lived out in the country in Arkansas then, and we always imagined someone dumped her at our place. We had no idea where she came from or how old she was.

We already had a little dachshund, so we didn't need another dog. Or so we thought.

But every attempt to run her off failed. The seventy-pound pit bull and the dachshund became best buddies, albeit a rather funny-looking running pair. Scooter, who looked like Petey in the old "Spanky and Our Gang" shows, had adopted us and soon became an integral part of our family. Despite the reputation of her breed, there was never a dog who loved being with people more than her.

A year-and-a-half later, I accepted a new job in Abilene, Texas. Since she had been an outside dog living in the country and we were moving to the city, we decided to leave her in Arkansas.

But shortly before our move, our youngest boy – a seventh grader at the time – announced that if Scooter wasn't going to Texas, he wasn't either.

We brought them both.

On our move to Abilene, we stayed overnight at a motel in Mount Pleasant in East Texas which allowed pets to stay in the room.

It was to be Scooter's first night to spend inside. It definitely wasn't her last.

When we went to bed that night, the dachshund was at the foot of our bed – as always. The two boys were in the other bed, and Scooter was on the floor.

I was the first to awake the next morning and rose to see if she was still sleeping on the floor.

But no Scooter! I panicked. She was nowhere to be found.

Then I looked back at the boys asleep in their bed. Through the dim light of the morning sun through the crack in the curtains, I could see each boy, laying straight out his head on the pillow.

Laying between them – under the covers with her head on the pillow – was Scooter.

Where was a camera when you really needed one?

As I stood there laughing, Scooter opened one eye and gave me a look as if to say, "Hey, this new place called Texas is going to be all right."

For nearly 10 years, it was.

Whether it was laying in the sun or tapping her tail to greet me when I came home late at night from work, Scooter knew she had made a good move years ago in adopting us as her family and moving to Texas.

We're happy we were adopted, too. Thanks, Scooter. We'll miss you.

———

Here was the feature story written by "Scooter, Al Pickett's best friend" (maybe with a little help by Greg Jaklewicz) on Jan. 4, 1991 in the *Reporter-News*:

After almost seven years of living with a sports editor, it's doggone time someone asked me for my opinion on football.

The Showcase folks have given me the opportunity to ask a

few pertinent questions of my own. Like why don't any National Football League teams have "dog" nicknames? At least, the Cleveland Browns have the "Dog Pound" at Municipal Stadium. Remember when the Patriots were from Boston and not New England? I thought they should've been called the Terriers.

Why not the Pittsburgh Pit Bulls? or the Dallas Dobermans? It's a howling shame.

No problem on the high school level – my favorite teams are Wylie, Clyde, Stamford and Coahoma. Love those Bulldogs.

College? Why, I like Pitt, of course. And I'm sure glad the Washington Huskies won the Rose Bowl.

Meanwhile, back to the question at paw, er, hand. How to watch the NFL playoffs this weekend:

First of all, have plenty of food and drink close by. It doesn't make any difference what kind of food – I'll eat anything that people eat. Al always has popcorn, but maybe he'll come up with a party tray this year.

Have a favorite, comfortable place to watch the game. Al likes the recliner, but I'm partial to the floor. Right on front of the recliner. Close to the food.

Have the Reporter-News sports section close by, too, so you'll know for sure what channels the games are on. You'll also want to see the sports guys' picks. That's usually worth a few laughs, especially Al's weekly boners.

Finally, my picks. I've sniffed out the winners, though I may be barking up a wrong tree or two.

In Saturday's wild-card games, I think Philadelphia will hound Washington, although I hope it turns out the other way. The Eagles' Bubby Ryan looks like a guy who would come home and kick his dog. Grrrrr....

I like Kansas City in the other game Saturday with Miami. It ought to be a close one – Dan Marino sure can bark out those signals – but the Chiefs should scratch out a win.

On Sunday, I'm picking the Houston Oilers to chew up Cincinnati and the Chicago Bears will beat the dog out of New Orleans.

And my favorites to reach the Super Bowl? I've bet two bones and a chew stick with the Irish Setter two blocks away on the San Francisco 49ers and Buffalo Bills.

The winner of Super Bowl XXV? I'll howl with delight if the 49ers win.

Those are my picks. It's time to get back to my busy schedule. I've got to lick clean the breakfast cereal bowl, take a mid-morning nap and bark at the neighbor's cat. But, I'll have my work done in time to watch the games on Saturday and Sunday.

Most Memorable Game

I am often asked what I would consider the most memorable game I have covered. That is difficult, but I think one game stands out – not just for the game itself, which was incredible, but for the circumstances surrounding it.

I didn't cover very many Razorback games during my nine years in Arkansas. It was about a four-hour drive from where I lived to Fayetteville, and most of the time I was covering high school or Harding University football or basketball games at the same time the Razorbacks were playing.

But on a Sunday afternoon, Feb. 12, 1984, I drove to Pine Bluff to cover a nationally televised basketball game between North Carolina and Arkansas. The Tar Heels were the defending national champion and were 19-0 and ranked No. 1 in the nation. NBC had scheduled a number of interesting, non-conference matchups in the middle of the conference races for Sunday afternoons back then, and the Arkansas-North Carolina tilt was one of those most highly anticipated games.

There were stars aplenty on both teams. North Carolina, coached by Dean Smith, featured Michael Jordan, Brad Daugherty and Sam Perkins, all future NBA stars. Eddie Sutton's Razorbacks had their own talented weapons, too, led by future NBA players Joe Kleine and Alvin Robertson.

The state's Associated Press Sports Editors Association had scheduled a meeting for that morning in the Pine Bluff Convention Center, prior to the game. It was a very interesting meeting because Dick Enberg and Al McGuire, the talented NBC broadcast team, took time away from their pregame preparations to speak to us.

I remember the colorful McGuire praising Enberg, noting that everyone who worked with Enberg became stars. He cited Merlin Olsen, who worked with Enberg on the National Football League telecasts. Certainly, McGuire was the most popular figure in college basketball at that time.

What made the matchup even more intriguing was that North Carolina had flown into Pine Bluff the day before the game, but Arkansas, the home team, couldn't get there until several hours before tipoff. Arkansas had played Southern Methodist University in Dallas in a Southwest Conference game the day before. The Razorbacks usually flew to their Southwest Conference games in Texas on several small planes provided by boosters, dubbed the "Razorback Air Force."

A line of severe thunderstorms and heavy rain, however, prevented the Arkansas team from flying into Pine Bluff following its Saturday afternoon game in Dallas. So the Razorbacks didn't arrive in Pine Bluff until shortly before the game. In fact, there had been some speculation that the team might not even be able to make it all because it was still raining hard in Pine Bluff.

The team did arrive on time, however, and when the Hogs came out for an early shootaround before the game, the arena was still empty except for the NBC television crew and a group of us sports writers who had come early for the APSE meeting.

Charles Balentine was an unheralded six-foot-six-inch senior forward from Newport, Arkansas, for the Razorbacks. I had covered Charles in high school and had actually brought him in to speak at a banquet a couple of years earlier.

When the team came out for its shootaround, Charles saw me across the court and came over to say hello.

"Did you just get here?" I asked him.

"Yeah, it was awful," he said. "We were bouncing, flying in and out of the thunderstorms and guys were sick on the plane."

Once it came time for tipoff, the sellout crowd of 7,529 packed into the Pine Bluff Convention Center was in a frenzy. Fans were roaring from start to finish and they were treated to a tremendous back-and-forth game. I had a prime seat with a photographer's pass, sitting on the floor next to the North Carolina cheerleaders.

Jordan led North Carolina with 21 points, while Kleine had 20 for the Hogs. Neither team led by more than seven points. The game came down to the final seconds with North Carolina leading 64-63.

But Balentine, the young man I had visited with just a couple of hours earlier, hit a short baseline jumper with four seconds left to put Arkansas up 65-64. North Carolina guard Steve Hale missed a shot from the corner – right in front of where I was seated – at the buzzer, and the arena went crazy. Arkansas had knocked off the nation's No. 1-ranked team in one of the most memorable games in Razorback history.

I went to the Arkansas locker room after the game, which, as you can imagine, was jubilant chaos.

"Great game," I told Charles as we reconnected.

"It is the greatest day of my life," Balentine shouted with a grin that couldn't be wiped off his face. Balentine finished with ten points that day, but his one baseline jumper cemented his place in Razorback lore forever.

The other thing I remember from that day was how gracious North Carolina coach Dean Smith was in face of the heartbreaking loss. A class act.

A chance to meet Dick Enberg and Al McGuire, the opportunity to be courtside for an upset of the nation's No. 1-ranked team, and the thrill of seeing Balentine, whom I considered a friend, be the hero, made that the most memorable game I covered in my fifty-year career.

———

Another game that stands out, not as a most memorable

but maybe the craziest game I ever broadcast, was a Hardin-Simmons University football game on October 27, 2012.

The Cowboys were playing Sul Ross State at Shelton Stadium in Abilene, Texas, and Hardin-Simmons beat the Lobos 86-42. The two teams combined for 1,714 yards total offense that day. That is still the most yards by two teams in a college football game in history.

I don't remember specifics of that game. I just remember that every time Hardin-Simmons would score and seemingly be ready to put in its reserves, Sul Ross would score on a big play and the Cowboys had to keep their starters in as the score got a little too close for comfort.

I don't remember, but I am assuming I didn't do a complete scoring recap in my postgame wrapup. That might have taken as long as the game itself.

Coaches and Good Friends

Al and Hardin-Simmons football coach Jesse Burleson taping their weekly coach's show.

As a sports writer and sportscaster for fifty years, I dealt with hundreds of coaches, many of whom became good friends.

When I left the newspaper world and began hosting a sports talk show on the radio in 2003, I taped a weekly coach's show with the football coaches from the three public high schools and the three universities in Abilene, Texas.

Although my radio show ended in 2020, a victim of COVID

and a lack of local advertising for the radio station, I still tape a televised weekly coach's show with Hardin-Simmons University head football coach Jesse Burleson that runs on that school's web site as well as the pregame on the livestream telecast of the Cowboys' games.

This is the story of how I met three of the many successful coaches I have been privileged to work with and who became good friends:

———

My first day on the job at the *Abilene Reporter-News* was the Tuesday before the first high school football game of the season in 1986. I was trying to meet as many people I could as the newcomer in town, so I went to the "Meet the Bulldogs Night" at Abilene Wylie High School.

There I met Wylie's newly named head football coach Hugh Sandifer. His guest speaker that night was Gordon Wood, a Wylie graduate who had just retired at Brownwood as the winningest high school football coach in the nation.

Imagine that, I met Hugh Sandifer and Gordon Wood on my first day in Abilene. My career was off and running, although I am not sure either Sandifer or I had a clue what the future would hold.

Sandifer first took a job teaching and coaching at Wylie in 1978. He was engaged to be married, but his future wife Brenda was studying in France while completing her degree in French from Abilene Christian University.

"I wrote her a letter and described where Wylie was, on the road to Buffalo Gap," Sandifer recalled. "But I said, 'Don't worry, I'll only be there a year and then I'll get a real job.'"

Well, that one year turned into forty-one and Wylie's football stadium in now renamed Hugh Sandifer Stadium.

Sandifer started out coaching eighth grade football, junior varsity basketball and high school boys and girls tennis at Wylie before being named the head boys basketball coach in 1982. In 1986, he was named the head football coach and athletic director, although he continued to coach both football and basketball until 1995, something almost unheard of for a school that size.

"I only planned to do it (coach both sports) for two or three years," Sandifer said, "but then I couldn't decide what I wanted to give up. I finally decided that if I was going to stay AD (athletic director), head football coach was a better fit."

In forty-one years, Sandifer watched Wylie grow from a little country school with all twelve grades on one campus to a Class 5A school with more than 1,300 students in high school alone. The one constant in the continuing growth, however, was the success of the athletic programs headed up by Sandifer.

In his thirteen years as the Wylie boys basketball coach, the Bulldogs posted a record of 231-132 and won six district titles. Sandifer was 285-109-4 as the head football coach, leading the Bulldogs to the state championship game four times and winning it all with a 17-14 win over Cuero in 2004.

Wylie enjoyed great success in other sports as well, winning multiple state titles in volleyball, girls basketball, baseball, golf and team tennis.

Sandifer retired in 2020, ending a remarkable career, all at Wylie High School. During that time, Sandifer said he coached a number of children of parents that he had coached earlier. That included our family as he coached both of our boys and my grandson.

———

Jimmie Keeling is a legend in Texas coaching circles and has been selected to a number of halls of fame. He posted a 182-125-12 record as a high school football coach, winning one state championship. He was then hired to start the football program from scratch at Hardin-Simmons University, compiling a remarkable 172-53 record over the next twenty years before retiring in 2010.

Coach Keeling and I became good friends, but, believe it or not, the first time we met was in a cemetery in Bangs, Texas. Keeling was the head football coach at San Angelo Central in 1988. A friend and sports writer at the *San Angelo Standard Times* was killed in a car wreck. I went to Bangs to attend the graveside services in his hometown, and there I met Keeling for the first time.

I remember thinking at the time how impressed I was that a

coach would go out of his way to attend the graveside services of a sports writer. Little did I know that in a year or two our lives would become intertwined.

I was there for the press conference when Keeling was named the head coach at Hardin-Simmons to start the Cowboys' football program. From 1990-2001, I covered the Cowboys for the newspaper and then in 2003 began broadcasting the HSU games on the radio,

Starting a new program was nothing new for Keeling, however. In 1967, he was hired to be the first football coach at Lubbock Estacado High School, which would be the first integrated school in Lubbock. The Matadors, with no seniors, played a junior varsity schedule that fall, and then the next year, in 1968, played its first season of varsity football.

Estacado went 14-0 and won a state championship, the only school in Texas to win a state championship in its first year of varsity football.

The players on that team wanted Keeling to write a book about their remarkable season. He enlisted me, and I wrote "Mighty, Mighty Matadors" that came out in 2018, the fiftieth anniversary of Estacado's state championship season. It was a great story about how student-athletes of all different backgrounds – brown, black, and white – came together for their unbelievable season. I was honored to be able to save the story of that historical season for posterity.

Hundreds of high school coaches around the state owe the

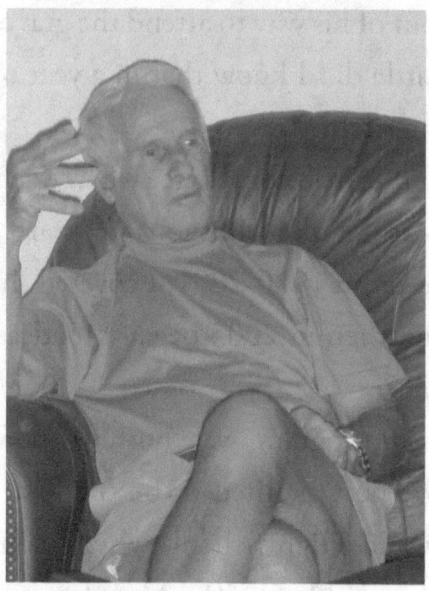

Emory Bellard being interviewed by Al
for his book, Wishbone Wisdom. (below)

start of their careers to Keeling. None of them, however, met him for the first time in a cemetery. I hold that distinction.

———

Another coach I became close to was Emory Bellard. We became acquainted when he was inducted into the Big Country Athletic Hall of Fame. Bellard won Texas high school state championships at Breckenridge and San Angelo Central before becoming the offensive coordinator for Darrell Royal at the University of Texas.

It was at Texas where the Longhorns unveiled what became known as the wishbone offense. Bellard later served as the head coach at Texas A&M and Mississippi State.

Coach Bellard always wanted a book written to tell the remarkable story of his life and how he invented the wishbone offense. So he and I spent several years together, recording interviews. I wrote it in Emory's voice, so it was described as "Wishbone Wisdom" by Emory Bellard as told to Al Pickett. It was published in 2010.

I will never forget when he and I went to the library in Breckenridge, where Bellard won state championships in 1958 and 1959. It was one of our first book signings, and there was already a line out of the door when we arrived.

I remember calling my brother later to tell him I finally found out how to sell books: Go to a town with a coach where he won a state championship. They loved him.

One of those there that day to get his autographed book was Shackelford County judge Ross Montgomery, who was a star running back at Midland when Bellard was coaching in San Angelo. Montgomery later played at Texas Christian University and with the Chicago Bears.

"I got a new deer rifle because of you," Bellard told a puzzled Montgomery.

Bellard went on to explain he had been asked in a preseason press conference how he was going to slow down that Montgomery kid from Midland.

"The only way I know to stop him is with a deer rifle," Bellard quipped.

The Bobcats beat Montgomery and Midland that year, and Bellard said the San Angelo Central booster club gave him a deer rifle as a present.

Coach Bellard and I spent the next six months doing book signings in Georgetown, Abilene, San Angelo and College Station, as well as Breckenridge, getting him the chance to reacquaint with many of his former players. But in July of that year, he was diagnosed with ALS. In February 2011, just a year after we published the book, he passed away.

I still consider it a great blessing that I got the book done in time for Coach Bellard to be able to do a number of book signings and see many of his old players and friends around the state.

Friday Nights
at Shotwell

I spent many a Friday night in the fall for more than thirty years at Shotwell Stadium in Abilene, Texas. It has perhaps the most unique and colorful history of any high school football stadium in Texas. If when the band plays the national anthem followed by the kickoff at Shotwell doesn't get your blood pumping, you probably don't live in West Texas.

In fact, two movies were filmed at Shotwell. The "Friday Night Lights" movie features scenes from an Abilene High-Odessa Permian game. I am a little unrecognizable dot looking out the press box window during a long shot of the press box in the movie, but I could spot where I was sitting. I later got to play myself as one of the announcers in a re-creation of the Abilene High-Cedar Hill game in the movie "Under the Stadium Lights" based on the book "Brother's Keeper" that I wrote about Abilene High's 2009 state championship season.

It is a great place to watch a game. Built as primarily a football-only stadium, there is no track around the football field, so the stands are close to the field for great viewing.

Built in 1959, Shotwell was modeled after Rice Stadium in Houston, which was host to Super Bowl VIII in 1974. Each of the stadium's two grandstands has a permanent seating capacity of 7,500 in an all-bleacher configuration. It was unique when it was built because it was an all-concrete stadium. Several semi-permanent metal bleacher structures are located behind the north end zone, allowing for overflow seating in excess of the facility's 15,000 permanent seats. Standing-room only areas at the corners of the stadium raise the potential total capacity to nearly 20,000, making it one of the larger high school stadiums in the state.

Texas boasts numerous magnificent high school football stadiums today, but Shotwell was one of the first. Artificial turf, new restrooms and locker rooms, and paved parking lots were added in 2002, but otherwise the stadium doesn't look much different than it did when it was built more than sixty-five years ago. In 2007, a $479,080 40-foot-wide, 34-foot-tall scoreboard featuring a 14-foot-wide by 24-foot-tall high-definition video screen that displays instant replays, messages and advertising, complete with sound, was installed on the north end, making Shotwell one of only a few high school stadiums in Texas to have two scoreboards. A new press box with an elevator and air conditioning was added in 2023.

Shotwell has hosted a number of state championship football games and hundreds of high school playoff games in its sixty-five-year-plus history, thanks to Abilene's central location between West Texas and the Panhandle and Central and North Texas. The stadium has seen more than its share of remarkable finishes and incredible accomplishments.

Although the highlight of the football season each year is the "Crosstown Showdown" between Abilene High and Cooper, which is usually played before a full house, Shotwell Stadium enjoys perhaps the most colorful and diverse history of any high school stadium in Texas.

World Series champions, Super Bowl winners and state champions have all played on the turf at Shotwell. The longest field goal in the history of football was also kicked in Shotwell when Swedish-born Ove Johansson of Abilene Christian University booted a sixty-nine-yard field goal against East Texas State on October 16, 1976. That record still stands.

The stadium even once hosted an American Football League exhibition game featuring two Hall of Fame coaches. The New York Titans (now the Jets) and Dallas Texans (now the Kansas City Chiefs) played an exhibition game at Shotwell in 1960. The two head coaches in that game– Sam Baugh and Hank Stram – are both the in Pro Football Hall of Fame.

An ill-fated college football bowl game, the Pecan Bowl, was held at Shotwell for a couple of years in the 1960s. The Fellowship of Christian Athletes organization has held its annual high school all-star game there each summer. The Abilene Convention and Visitors Bureau once hosted the "Champions

Classic" at Shotwell, even attracting out-of-state high school football teams to the event which raised money for college scholarships. Abilene Wylie, which is its own independent school district and has its own Hugh Sandifer Stadium, has also played several playoff games at Shotwell.

Abilene Christian University called Shotwell its home stadium from 1959 until it opened its new on-campus Wildcat Stadium in 2017. All three local colleges have played in Shotwell Stadium at one time or another. In fact, the highest-scoring NCAA Division II game in history was played in the stadium. ACU beat West Texas A&M 93-68 in a playoff game in 2008.

First a little history: How did Shotwell get its unusual name?

When it was built in 1959, it was called Abilene Public Schools Stadium. Shortly after that first season, however, it was renamed Shotwell Stadium after P.E. "Pete" Shotwell, a long-time football coach at Abilene High School. In fact, it was the first facility in the Abilene Independent School District to be named for someone who was still living.

Shotwell was the first coach in Texas high school history to win state championships at three different high schools. He began his coaching career at Cisco in 1916 and a couple of years later moved to Abilene. His 1923 Eagles went 12-0 and won a state championship with one of the strongest defensive performances ever, allowing only one touchdown by an opponent during the entire season.

Shotwell coached for two years at Simmons College (now Hardin-Simmons University) in Abilene and one year at Sul Ross State in Alpine before returning to the high school ranks. He won a state championship at Breckenridge in 1929 and captured another at Longview in 1937. He returned to Abilene in 1946 and coached the Abilene High Eagles until 1952. Shotwell then served as the athletic director at McMurry College (now McMurry University) from 1959-72. He died in 1978.

Although the stadium is named for Shotwell, it could certainly be considered the "House that Moser Built." Chuck Moser, a native of Missouri and an all-conference center at the University of Missouri who came to Texas to serve during World War II, was hired from McAllen to replace Shotwell in 1953.

In seven years as the head coach at Abilene High, Moser's Eagles won six consecutive district championships, three straight state titles and had a nation-best 49-game winning streak from 1953-57. The *Dallas Morning News* in 1999 named Moser's Eagles the Texas high school "Team of the Century." The 15,000-seat stadium was a tribute to the remarkable success that Moser's teams enjoyed.

Moser's final season was 1959, the first year of the new stadium. The next year, Cooper opened, making Abilene a two-high-school town, and Moser became the athletic director for the school district, a job he held for 14 years before taking an assistant coaching position at Texas A&M.

The first game played in the new Public Schools Stadium in 1959 certainly proved to be forerunner of things to come, not only for exciting finishes but also for future stars that played there.

Abilene High edged San Antonio Jefferson 14-12 in the first game in the new stadium. The star of the game was the Eagles wide receiver David Parks, who went on to a stellar career at Texas Tech. In 1964 the San Francisco 49ers made Parks the No. 1 pick in the National Football League draft. Parks finished runner-up for the NFL Rookie of the Year. He played four seasons with the 49ers before signing with New Orleans. After five seasons with the Saints, Parks played one year for the Houston Oilers before finishing his 11-year professional football career with the Southern California Sun in the World Football League.

San Antonio Jefferson's roster included sophomore linebacker Tommy Nobis. In 1966, two years after Parks was the first pick in the NFL draft, the Atlanta Falcons selected Nobis, a two-time all-American at the University of Texas, with the No. 1 pick. Nobis, like Parks, enjoyed an 11-year career in the NFL, all with the Falcons. Nobis was the 1966 NFL Rookie of the Year. Parks and Nobis are members of the Texas Tech and University of Texas halls of fame, respectively, and are members of the Texas Sports Hall of Fame. Sadly, Nobis died in 2017 and Parks in 2019 after each suffered dementia possibly resulting from chronic traumatic encephalopathy.

So the first game ever played in Shotwell Stadium featured two players who each became the very first selection in the NFL draft, a remarkable feat that has not since been repeated.

Abilene High quarterback Charles McCook, who later became a dentist in Post, holds the distinction of scoring the first touchdown in the new stadium. McCook's three-yard run with 2:24 left in the second quarter and Bobby Austin's extra-point kick gave the Eagles a 7-0 lead.

Seconds later, Abilene recovered a fumble, and the Eagles used a trick play for another score. McCook threw a ten-yard pass to Parks, who lateraled back to Sarge Newman on a hook-and-lateral play. Newman ran for a touchdown, completing the forty-four-yard play with 1:51 remaining.

Abilene's 14-0 halftime lead held up – barely. Jefferson scored two second-half touchdowns, but Parks recovered a fumble on the two-point conversion try that would have tied the game.

On the Thursday following the Eagles' opener, Hardin-Simmons University faced North Texas State in the first collegiate game played in the new stadium. Like the Abilene High-San Antonio Jefferson contest, HSU's game against North Texas also featured a future pro star. Running back Abner Haynes led North Texas State to a 46-24 romp over the Cowboys before a crowd of 11,500. Haynes rushed for 4,630 yards and 20 touchdowns, caught 287 passes for 3,535 yards and scored a pair of touchdowns on punt and kickoff returns during an eight-year AFL career with the Dallas Texans, Kansas City Chiefs, Miami Dolphins and New York Jets.

Hardin-Simmons was coached by Sam Baugh, the Sweetwater native and legendary Washington Redskins quarterback who was in his final season as the HSU head coach before leaving to become the first head coach of the New York Titans (Jets) in 1960.

Although I covered so many great games and great moments at Shotwell over the years, one of my more memorable humorous memories occurred in 2004.

Abilene High and Cooper played back-to-back overtime games in 2003 and 2004, two of the great games in the history of the "Crosstown Showdown." The Eagles and Cougars were both ranked among the top five teams in the state in Class 5A going into the 2004 matchup.

It was a chilly, drizzling night, but an overflow crowd was packed into Shotwell Stadium for the much-anticipated matchup. It was the Friday night before the Tuesday general election, and Governor Rick Perry, who grew up in nearby Haskell, and Lt. Governor David Dewhurst were running for re-election. So not wanting to miss the chance to appear in front of more than 15,000 potential voters, the two came to Abilene to toss the opening coin.

Chuck Statler, my broadcast partner for Abilene High's

games, is a Taylor County commissioner for his day job, so he is connected with many of the state's politicians. During our pregame broadcast, his cell phone kept ringing, so he finally answered it.

It was an aide for Dewhurst, who said the Lt. Governor had just landed at Abilene Regional Airport and wanted to know how to get to the stadium.

For anyone who lives in Abilene, that is funny because you can see Shotwell Stadium from the airport. If you make a left out of the airport and turn on to Highway 36 headed for downtown Abilene, you drive right by the stadium. It is a drive that takes only two or three minutes.

"Turn left," Statler told him. "When you see the lights, all the cars and 15,000 people, you are there."

Politicians know when it is a "Big Game," even if they don't know how to get there.

———

Even though Shotwell has seen its share of amazing finishes, a 2024 district matchup between Abilene High and Amarillo Tascosa will certainly go down as one of the most unusual.

Tascosa, clinging to a 28-21 lead, had the ball inside its own ten-yard-line in the final seconds. Rather than risk having a punt blocked on fourth down, the Rebels decided to have its punter run out of the back of the end zone and take an automatic safety, seemingly a good strategic decision.

That cut Tascosa's lead to 28-23, but the Rebels still had a free kick from the twenty-yard line. Tascosa elected to kick it deep, and speedy Ryland Bradford raced sixty-five yards for a game-winning touchdown and an improbable 29-28 Abilene High victory.

———

Finally, I saw something in a football game at Shotwell Stadium in the 1990s that I wouldn't have believed if I hadn't seen it myself.

A blue norther blew in shortly before a game between Abilene Cooper and Odessa Permian. With the cold, strong wind gusting, Permian attempted an extra point in the north end of the stadium. The high floating kick went through the uprights and then blew back, landing in the end zone just a yard or two from the goal line.

The officials correctly ruled the PAT was good because it went through the uprights, but have you ever seen a successful kick blow back and actually hit the ground in the end zone after clearing the crossbar?

Controversial Field Goal and Other Tough Losses

Hardly a weekend goes by that you don't see a high school, college or National Football League game decided by last-second field goal.

Usually, a team that is tied or down by just one, two or three points, works itself into field-goal range and then calls its final timeout to set up its potential game-winning or tying field goal.

But have you ever seen a team run its field-goal team on to the field just in time to kick a game-winner? It doesn't happen very often, but I broadcast a game in which it happened.

Did the team get the kick off in time? I don't know, but I think so. Did the officials handle the final play right? I don't know, but I don't think so.

Let's set the stage to understand the controversial finish: Mary Hardin-Baylor and Hardin-Simmons have typically been ranked among the top teams in the nation in NCAA Division

III over the last twenty-five years. The series has developed into quite a rivalry between the two Texas Baptist-affiliated schools. One or the other has won or shared the American Southwest Conference title every year since 1998.

When the two teams met at Crusader Stadium in Belton, Texas, in 2019, Mary Hardin-Baylor was the defending national champion and ranked number one in the nation. Hardin-Simmons, however, held a 14-12 lead late in the game thanks to two missed extra points and a missed field goal by Mary Hardin-Baylor.

Both teams were out of timeouts, but the Cru was driving into HSU territory. On third down, Mary Hardin-Baylor completed a pass over the middle to its tight end who was tackled immediately at the twenty-five-yard-line, four yards short of the needed yardage for a first down.

The Cru quickly lined up to run a play. But they then realized they couldn't spike the ball to stop the clock because it was fourth down. So the offensive team ran off the field and the field-goal unit raced out to try a field goal.

Mary Hardin-Baylor was driving toward the south end of Crusader Stadium. The scoreboard and big video board is in the north end of the stadium. As the offense ran off the field and the field-goal unit came out, I turned to look at the scoreboard and began counting down the seconds on my broadcast:

"Eight, seven, six, five, four, three."

When it clicked to two seconds, I turned back to see Mary

Hardin-Baylor lined up to try the field goal. Then the Cru snapped the ball and Anthony Villa nailed a forty-two-yard field goal to win the game 15-14.

Did he get the kick off in time? I assume so, because the back judge who is in charge of keeping track of the clock would have been facing the scoreboard. But I can't say for sure since I was watching the play, not the scoreboard. But if he did get the kick off in time, it had to be by just a fraction of a second.

Did the officials handle the final play correctly? Hardin-Simmons coach Jesse Burleson doesn't think so. He was trying to substitute in a tall pass rusher to try to block the kick.

"The umpire said he held them (the offense) for three seconds," Burleson said later. "But that is not the rule."

Under college football rules today, the umpire is required to hold up play until the defense can make its substitution to counter the offense's alignment. I watched a game on television recently where the defensive team was slow in getting a substitute on to the field, forcing the offense to take timeout rather than suffer a delay-of-game penalty.

Mary Hardin-Baylor had lined up with its offensive unit before changing its mind and running its field-goal unit on to the field. It would seem to me that Hardin-Simmons should have had time to make its defensive substitution. Coach Burleson certainly believed so.

Instead, it goes down as one of the most gut-wrenching losses in Hardin-Simmons football history.

Losses like the Hardin-Simmons game at Mary Hardin-Baylor are tough to take, especially when your team seemingly has the game won only to have the rug pulled out from beneath it in the final seconds.

It happened twice to Abilene High – in back-to-back years – in playoff games I was broadcasting.

In 2015, the Eagles appeared to be in position to upset Arlington Lamar and quarterback Shane Beuchele – who went on to play at Texas, SMU and a backup for the Kansas City Chiefs – in a bi-district playoff game. Abilene High's Oscar Garcia booted a thirty-nine-yard field goal with eleven seconds remaining to take a 33-32 lead.

The Eagles, however, elected to kick deep on the ensuing kickoff, and Lamar's Draven Cantly returned it ninety-eight yards for a game-winning touchdown, crossing the goal line with three seconds left and giving Lamar a 39-33 victory.

Oddly enough, Abilene High coach Del Van Cox never saw the game-winning kickoff return. He had torn his Achilles heel earlier and had to wear a boot on his foot. So for the first time in his career, he was coaching from the press box rather than the sideline.

"I never saw it," Cox recalled. "When we kicked the field goal, I got on the elevator to come down to the field."

As tough as that loss was to Arlington Lamar, a third-round

playoff loss the next year in 2016 was even harder to swallow.

DeSoto, ranked No. 2 in the state, and Abilene High locked horns in a wild shootout. DeSoto scored with less than two minutes remaining to pull to within three, 45-42. Abilene High's Wes Berry recovered the ensuing onside kick, so the Eagles just had to run the clock out to pull off the monumental upset. They needed only one more first down before being able to take a knee and pull off the huge upset.

"We were trying to run out the clock," Cox said. "I still have nightmares seeing our quarterback lying on the ground."

AHS quarterback Peyton Killam carried the ball around the right side when he was tackled. While he was lying on the ground, a DeSoto player stripped the ball away from him. Replays showed Killam was clearly already down on the turf when the ball was stripped from him. But the officials ruled it a fumble. DeSoto then drove for a touchdown with forty-eight seconds left to claim a 49-45 victory.

DeSoto went on to capture the Class 6A Division II state championship, and Abilene High was left to wonder what might have been except for a questionable fumble call.

Defeat snatched the jaws of victory are always tough to take.

———

Sometimes, however, the tables turn and your team claims a win that seemed unlikely. Such was the case for Abilene High in 2007.

In the early 2000s, Abilene High was just starting its run as one of the state's top football teams. But powerhouse Southlake Carroll was seemingly standing in the Eagles' way, handing Abilene High third-round playoff losses in 2004 and 2005 en route to winning state championships.

Those Abilene High teams were led by quarterback Taylor Potts, who went on to an outstanding career at Texas Tech. Southlake Carroll, however, had quarterbacks Chase Daniel and Greg McElroy in 2004 and 2005, respectively. Daniel played at Missouri and McElroy at Alabama. Both went on to play in the NFL, and McElroy became a football commentator on national television.

In 2007, the Eagles and Dragons met again in the third round, this time at Texas Stadium in Irving. Abilene High rallied from a 21-9 deficit to take a 22-21 lead, but Southlake Carroll was driving for a potential game-winning field goal, reaching the ten-yard-line in the closing seconds. The Dragons were in position to attempt a chip-shot field goal but decided to run one more play to apparently center the ball in the middle of the field before calling their final timeout.

Southlake Carroll's quarterback, going under center for the first time in the game instead of being in the shotgun formation, fumbled the snap, however. Abilene High recovered the fumble and was able to take a knee on one final play to escape with its first win over Southlake Carroll.

I actually missed the fumble. Network television and

national radio broadcasters have statisticians, spotters and an engineer. In local radio broadcasts, the two of us handle all of those duties. I kept stats during the game, worked without a spotter and did our own engineering. I was quickly adding up the stats in anticipation of Southlake Carroll handing Abilene High another heartbreaking loss.

So when my broadcast partner Chuck Statler hollered "fumble," I looked up to see the Abilene High sideline in a wild celebration. It ended Southlake Carroll's run of three consecutive Class 5A Division II state championships. And two years later, Abilene High finally climbed to the summit, capturing its first state championship in fifty-three years.

It was a thrill to be there for the upset of Southlake Carroll and Abilene High's entire unbeaten 2009 state championship season, even if I did miss the "fumble."

State Championships

*Al and fellow Abilene High broadcaster Chuck Statler
during the filming of the Under the Stadium Lights movie.*

If you are covering high school sports, there is nothing bigger
than a state championship game. In Texas high school football

these days, that means finishing the season at the spectacular 100,000-seat AT&T Stadium in Arlington, home of the Dallas Cowboys and the 60-yard-wide video board.

It is the dream of all Texas high school football players to make it to AT&T Stadium. How big is high school football in Texas?

There are currently twelve state championship games played over four days at AT&T Stadium. In 2021, for example, those twelve games drew more than 214,000 fans (in the middle of a pandemic), not to mention all twelve games were televised statewide on Bally Sports Southwest.

In 2009, however, the playoffs for Abilene High began at AT&T Stadium. That was the first year that AT&T Stadium opened, and most fans hadn't been there to see the $1.2 billion stadium in person. They had only watched the Dallas Cowboys on television.

Abilene High had been placed in District 3-5A, a Fort Worth-area district, for the first time a year earlier instead of its traditional West Texas district. District 3-5A and District 4-5A, an Arlington-Mansfield district, made an agreement to play its four first-round bi-district playoff games at AT&T Stadium. Those would be the first high school games to be played in the new stadium, and fans turned out in huge numbers to get their first look at "Jerry World."

There were two games scheduled on Thursday night and two more on Friday. Abilene High drew the first game on Friday against Arlington Lamar. So you can imagine how excited my broadcast partner Chuck Statler and I were to be able to broadcast only the third high school football game to ever be played in AT&T Stadium.

We made the necessary arrangements and arrived at the pass gate early, telling the lady working there that we had been assigned Booth 3. We told her we had no idea where Booth 3 was.

"I don't, either," she replied. "I will get someone to help you."

In just a few minutes, a very nice security official in a coat and tie arrived. He, too, said he wasn't sure where Booth 3 was, but he would take us there.

A quick trip up an elevator and he led us into the biggest booth I had ever been in. It was located right above the first level on the 50-yard line. It was a huge booth with an open room behind it and even had its own restroom.

I couldn't help but think back to my first year of broadcasting football. Like the night in Axtell, Kansas, where there wasn't enough room in the press box so they drove a pickup truck next to the field and set up a table and chair in the bed of the pickup for me.

Or the night in Holton, Kansas, where they said there wasn't enough room in the pressbox but they would put a table and chairs on the roof for us. That was fine, except it snowed during the game.

So we thought we had finally made the "big time" in this beautiful expansive booth and quickly began unpacking our equipment. The security guard was on his walkie-talkie as we began set up our equipment.

"Sorry, guys, but this isn't your booth," he interrupted us. "This is the Fox TV booth."

So we repacked our equipment and headed down to a "much smaller" booth in the corner behind the end zone. Joe Buck's and Troy Aikman's jobs were safe, but we had their seats – for at least a few minutes that day.

A year earlier, Abilene High had gone 10-0, only to be upset by Mansfield in the opening round, so we didn't really know what to expect. Plus, whenever Arlington Lamar lost it would probably be the final game for Eddie Peach, the only football coach Lamar had had since the school opened in 1970. He had won 311 games during his remarkable career at Lamar. It was rumored that he was going to announce his retirement at age sixty-seven at the end of the season. A few weeks later, he did just that.

We wondered what impact the emotion of Peach's impending retirement would have on the Lamar team. Abilene High, however, rolled to an impressive 42-10 victory over the Vikings.

At that point, we had no idea what was about to unfold over the next five weeks. The Eagles, who began the season unranked, kept rolling, knocking off the state's No. 1-ranked team Cedar Hill (coached by Joey McGuire, who became the head coach at Texas Tech) in the third round 42-17 and then beating two-time defending state champion Katy 28-10 in the Class 5A Division II state championship game in front of an estimated 30,000 fans in San Antonio's Alamodome as well as a statewide television audience. It was Abilene High's first state championship since 1956.

To broadcast every game during a 15-0 season that culminated in a state championship was one of the great thrills of my career. Team chaplain Chad Mitchell and I co-wrote a book "Brother's Keeper" about that season and in 2021, a movie "Under the Stadium Lights" based on the book was released.

So I got to relive that season over the next decade and even got to play myself as the announcer in the movie. Who would have dreamed a book and movie would follow that state championship?

———

There are two other state championship football games that stand out during my career as sports editor of the *Abilene Reporter-News*, but for different reasons.

Christmas fell on a Tuesday in 1990, and Munday, a small town some 80 miles north of Abilene, was scheduled to face Bartlett from Central Texas for the Class 1A state championship at Pennington Field in Bedford, located in the heart of the Dallas-Fort Worth Metroplex. The game was scheduled for the Saturday before Christmas, but a major ice storm hit Texas a day earlier.

Roads all across the state were nearly impassable. In fact, Munday couldn't even get out of town.

So the game was rescheduled for Monday afternoon, Christmas Eve. Bartlett won the game 36-28 on a chilly-but-sunny day, but the thing I remember most about that day was Santa Claus landing in the end zone in a helicopter during the pregame. I assume his reindeer were still resting up for their big night in a few hours.

Christmas Eve is typically the one day in which there are no sporting events, so I remember how strange it seemed as I made the three-hour trip back home to Abilene while the rest of my family was attending Christmas Eve services at church.

———

The other memorable state championship football game was memorable not for the game itself but who played in it.

Abilene Cooper had knocked off Richardson Lake Highlands in an overtime thriller in the semifinals and was set to face Austin Westlake for the 1996 Class 5A Division II state title at Texas Stadium in Irving. It was Cooper's first state championship game appearance since a Jack Mildren-led Cougars team had lost a controversial 20-19 decision to Austin Reagan in the 1967 state championship game.

Cooper and Westlake were tied 7-7 at halftime, but Westlake's quarterback lit up the Cougars' defense in the second half as the Chaparrals' rolled to a 55-15 victory. Who was that quarterback? Drew Brees, who, of course, went on to become one of the top passers in National Football League history with the New Orleans Saints.

So, I got my first look at Brees in a high school state championship game in 1996.

Throw A Flutie

November 23, 1984, is a memorable day in college football history. That was the day after Thanksgiving, and Boston College and No. 1-ranked University of Miami played a high-scoring game that afternoon in a nationally televised contest that drew a huge audience on CBS.

Miami had taken a 45-41 lead with less than a minute to play. But Boston College, led by quarterback Doug Flutie drove to the Hurricanes' 48-yard line. With six seconds left, Boston College had time for one last play. Flutie scrambled and heaved a "Hail Mary" pass that was caught in the end zone by Gerald Phelan to give Boston College the heart-stopping 47-45 victory.

Even Flutie agreed later that his performance and "Hail Mary" pass that day is what clinched his winning the Heisman Trophy.

That collegiate classic, however, is not what I remember from that day.

That night, Searcy hosted Harrison in the Arkansas Class 3A state semifinal at Lions Stadium. A win would vault Searcy into the state championship game for the first time in thirty years.

It was also the first time that I – or probably anyone else in the stadium that night – had ever seen an overtime football game.

Texas high schools play by NCAA rules, while Arkansas, and most other states, plays under National High School Federation rules. There are only a small number of differences in the two rules.

But in 1984, the national federation for the first time approved an overtime for high school football. It would be another year before the NCAA would adopt a similar overtime rule for college football games.

Unlike the NCAA rule that we all have become accustomed to in which each team gets a possession beginning at the 25-yard line, the federation rule in 1984 gave each team a possession in the overtime at their opponent's ten-yard line.

Searcy and Harrison finished regulation tied 14-14, so the two teams went to overtime with most of the fans in the packed stadium trying to figure out if they understood the new rule.

Searcy went first, and had a fifteen-yard clipping penalty on the first play. So it was now first-and-twenty-five. On the next play, Searcy's star quarterback Jimmy Simpson, who went on to play for the Arkansas Razorbacks, was sacked for a nine-yard loss. Now, it was second-and-thirty-four. An incomplete pass made it third-and-thirty-four.

On third down, Simpson heaved a pass to the end zone that was caught by Eric Clay for a thirty-four-yard touchdown. The ensuing extra point put the Lions up 21-14, but Harrison still had its possession.

Harrison was a power running team, and after three plays the Goblins had reached the one-yard line. On fourth-and-goal at the one, Harrison's running back plunged across for a touchdown, meaning an extra-point kick would send the game to a second overtime.

Harrison, however, elected to go for a two-point conversion to try to win the game. Harrison's coach was quoted later that his defense was so shell-shocked by giving up the long TD pass earlier, that he didn't want to send his defense out there again.

Harrison tried a roll-out pass for the two-point conversion try, but the pass bounced off the diving receiver's hands as he hit the turf, giving Searcy a dramatic 21-20 win and sending the Lions to the state title game at War Memorial Stadium in Little Rock.

Afterwards, I asked Simpson, who later became a lawyer in his hometown, about the game-winning pass.

"When I left the house to come to the game, the last thing my grandmother told me was to throw a 'Flutie' tonight," Simpson replied.

And he did.

'Too Small' Overachiever

If someone plays twelve seasons in the National Football League, earns five Pro Bowl selections, and leads the league in receptions three times, one would likely assume that player was considered a "blue-chip" top prospect coming out of high school.

Well, nothing could be further from the truth when one considers the remarkable career of Texas Tech's Wes Welker. A story I wrote once about how he became a Red Raider remains one of my favorites as an example of how recruiting is an inexact science. Sometimes there is more to consider than how tall, how fast, or how high he can jump. There is another factor called "heart" which apparently is difficult to measure.

Welker was named the *Daily Oklahoman's* Player of the Year as a senior at Heritage Hall High School in Oklahoma City. He rushed for 3,235 career yards and fifty-three touchdowns and caught 174 passes for 2,551 yards and twenty-seven touchdowns. He also returned fifty-eight career punts for 495 yards.

So college recruiters were knocking down his door to sign him, right? Wrong.

Despite those impressive statistics, Welker couldn't find a school that wanted him.

"I wasn't too highly recruited," he said in a 2002 interview with me. "My size and speed were big questions."

Welker was five-foot-nine with 4.5 speed, so college recruiters wanted someone taller or faster.

Rod Warner, Welker's high school coach at Heritage Hall, wasn't willing to sit back and let his star player get passed over, however.

"I kept telling coaches that you've got to look beyond his size and speed," said Warner. "He's a football player. He's like an assistant coach on the field. He's our career leading scorer and career leading tackler. I've coached a lot of kids in thirty years, and he's the best I've ever coached. His practice habit and loyalty are qualities you can't get from many kids today."

Warner remembered Welker returning in tears from a visit to the University of Tulsa when the Golden Hurricanes decided to offer a scholarship to another receiver with more speed.

"On the Saturday before signing day, I sent nearly 100 faxes to Division I colleges," Warner said. "I got calls back from Michigan, Illinois and Virginia Tech."

But no one was willing to make an offer.

Warner also called his old friend Tommy McVeigh, the

director of football operations at Texas Tech at the time. The two had coached together at Derby High School in Kansas in the mid-1970s.

"Tom said he thought they were full," Warner said, "but the next day I got a call back from Tom. He said they had a kid who may not come. He asked if it opens, would Wes be interested. I said sure; he doesn't have any other offers."

Then Tuesday, the night before National Signing Day, Warner was attending his daughter's high school basketball game in Stillwater when his cell phone rang. It was McVeigh.

"I went into a janitor's closet so I could hear," Warner said. "I talked to Tom and the receivers coach. I told everyone he's the best player I've coached."

On Thursday, the day after signing day, Texas Tech called and set up a visit for Welker to Lubbock that weekend.

"Wes's mom was a nervous wreck the whole time," Warner said. "Coach (Mike) Leach kept showing him around and talking about how he'd fit in, but he never made an offer. Finally, Coach Leach's cell phone rang while they were at lunch. When he hung up, Coach Leach said, 'If I offer today, how soon can you make a decision?' Wes said, 'How's right now? Is that soon enough?'"

And that is how Wes Welker became a Red Raider. So how did that work out for Texas Tech?

Over his four-year career, Welker had 259 receptions for 3,019 yards and twenty-one touchdowns, 341 kick return yards and seventy-nine rushes for 456 and two touchdowns. He set the NCAA record for punt return yards with 1,761 and returned eight punts for touchdowns in his career. In 2003, Walker won the Mosi Tatupu Award, given annually to the best special teams player in college football, and he was named first team all-Big 12. Walker was also named to the *Sports Illustrated* All-Decade Team as a punt returner.

Despite his amazing collegiate career, however, Welker was not invited to the NFL Scouting Combine and went undrafted. So he had to prove himself all over again.

He signed as a free agent with the San Diego Chargers but was cut after the first game. Welker then signed with Miami and played three years with the Dolphins, six seasons with the New England Patriots and his final three seasons with the Denver Broncos and St. Louis Rams.

Welker was a two-team first team all-Pro selection and a five-team Pro Bowl pick during his NFL career. His final NFL numbers include 903 receptions for 9,924 receiving yards and fifty receiving touchdowns as well as 6,722 return yards and one touchdown.

After coaching in the NFL, Welker is now a personnel analyst for his former Texas Tech quarterback Kliff Kingsbury, who is the offensive coordinator for the Washington Commanders.

It is the remarkable story of how Welker went from a too-small, too-slow athlete to become one of the top receivers in Big 12 and NFL history.

Travel Woes

When you read the game story in the newspaper the next day or listen to the radio broadcast or watch the telecast, probably the last thing you think about is what all went into making it possible to listen or watch the game or read about it in your paper the next morning.

One of those challenges is travel.

For those of us who live in West Texas, the distance to travel to cover high school games is something that I think those in metropolitan areas such as the Dallas-Fort Worth Metroplex can't comprehend. For example, Abilene High and Abilene Cooper spend much of their football, baseball and basketball schedules playing teams from Midland, Odessa, Lubbock or Wichita Falls, all of which are 150 to 180 miles away. Sometimes, they play teams from the Metroplex, which is the same distance the other direction, only with a lot more traffic.

In basketball, that often means a three-hour road trip on a Tuesday night, get home after midnight and back at school the next morning.

Recently, the Abilene schools have been placed in the same

football district with Amarillo schools. That is a 250-mile trip one way.

That meant many a night driving home at one or two in the morning after filing my story or wrapping up my broadcast. That was before Sirius radio, so I spent the night trying to find the 50,000-watt clear channel radio stations out of Denver or New Orleans. Anything to try to keep myself entertained – and awake.

In 2001, I drove 450 miles in a dust storm to El Paso for a bi-district football playoff and then a 450-mile drive back home after the game.

Weather, of course, can always be a challenge. I remember broadcasting a regional basketball tournament in Chapman, Kansas, in the early years of my career. What a surprise when I walked out of the gym that night to find a major snow storm had hit. My scheduled one-hour drive back home in a blizzard certainly took much longer than planned.

One of the biggest challenges was a weekend when I had a Friday night high school football broadcast in Odessa and a noon Saturday football broadcast with Hardin-Simmons University at Tyler College. Look at a map. That is approximately 450 miles from Odessa and to Tyler. And two hours of sleep for those keeping track.

Or there was the night I covered the Dallas Cowboys' playoff game at Texas Stadium in Irving. It was the first year that Jimmy Johnson got the Cowboys in the playoffs. The game was an

11:30 a.m. kickoff. By the time I did the postgame interviews in the locker room and filed my story, it was five o'clock and I was ready for the three-hour drive back home to Abilene.

When I stopped in Weatherford to get a Coke, it was starting to mist. The temperature was just right, the mist was freezing on the road. The farther west I went, the slicker the road became and the slower I could drive.

Fortunately, TxDot had sanded Ranger Hill, so I was able to navigate that treacherous steep incline that was often the site of wrecks during bad weather.

My speed slowed from sixty to forty to twenty miles per hour as I continued my trip. When I reached the Clyde rest area on Interstate 20, some fifteen miles from Abilene, there was a semi jack-knifed in the median and a TxDot truck was stopped and trying to spread sand under the big tractor-trailer rig to get it moving again.

I remember thinking to myself, that surely wasn't the only TxDot sand truck on the road. It was!

The last stretch home was at ten miles per hour. Twelve mph was too fast, causing the car to slide.

When I walked into the house at 10:15 p.m.,. more than two hours after I was scheduled to be home, my wife said, "I was starting to get worried about you."

"You were worried," I replied. "I was scared to death out there."

———

But my "road trip from hell" as I like to describe it, didn't involve driving. Instead, it was a rare flight.

Louisiana College (now known as Louisiana Christian) in Pineville, La., was in the American Southwest Conference with Hardin-Simmons University back then. We had always made the eight-hour drive to Pineville.

But one year, Hardin-Simmons athletic director John Neese decided we would fly. What a great idea to not have to spend sixteen hours on the road in a weekend. Our normal traveling party was Neese, sports information director Chad Grubbs and Tim McCary from Hardin-Simmons and my broadcast partner Phil Ashby.

Our plan was to fly to Shreveport, eat a nice lunch and then make the two-hour drive to Pineville for the 6 p.m. kickoff. We would then drive back to Shreveport and catch the early morning flight the next day. We would be back home before noon on Sunday. It was great plan.

I had a high school football broadcast in the Dallas-Fort Worth area on Friday night, so I met the rest of the crew at DFW International Airport the next morning. They had flown in from Abilene.

At 10 a.m. as we were scheduled to board the plane for a short forty-five minute flight to Shreveport, a thunderstorm sat right over the airport, shutting down all flights.

We quickly rebooked to the 11 a.m. flight and then again to

the noon flight. But by this time, a line of heavy thunderstorms was stretching from Dallas to Chicago and no flights were coming in or going out.

So we rented a car and drove like crazy, often through heavy rain, to get to Pineville. Our pregame show was scheduled to begin at 5:30 p.m., but we arrived at the stadium at 5:50 p.m., just in time to plug in our equipment, call the radio station and announce the kickoff.

Hardin-Simmons jumped out to a big lead, but, late in the first quarter, a thunderstorm hit. Lightning, thunder and rain coming sideways. The game was halted, but after a long delay, the game resumed. The Cowboys were leading 34-6 when another thunderstorm hit with less than three minutes remaining before halftime.

After another lengthy delay, it was decided to cancel the game. It was 10 p.m. We had kicked off at 6 p.m. and after four hours hadn't even gotten to halftime.

So we drove back to Shreveport. Our bags had flown to Shreveport, so when we got to the airport after midnight, it was closed. So we had to go to our motel when no contact cases, no toothbrushes, no change of clothes.

A quick night's sleep and we were back at the airport at 5 a.m. Our bags were there waiting for us, and we caught the 7 a.m. flight back to DFW. I was getting off there to meet my wife who was at our son's, while the rest of crew flew back to Abilene.

That was fine except American Eagle lost my bag between

Shreveport and Dallas. They flew it back to Abilene later. In fact, when we got home, my suitcase was waiting for me on the front porch.

Canceled flights, a lost bag and a wild drive all for a game that didn't happen. League rules said a game must complete three quarters before it could be declared an official game.

———

Sometimes, I am amazed to think about what college and professional teams go through with flights and buses to get to their games. In 2022, I got to witness what could go wrong.

I was flying with the Hardin-Simmons football team on a charter flight (from a company in Florida that specializes in flying athletic teams on charter flights) out of Abilene to Madison, Wisconsin. The team was then going to bus seventy miles to Platteville for a game this next day against Wisconsin-Platteville. The team was staying across the river from Platteville in Dubuque, Iowa.

The team had booked a bus company out of Chicago to provide the transportation to Platteville. When we arrived in Madison, however, there were no buses waiting.

The assistant coach, who had the travel assignment, called the bus company.

"We have had a breakdown," he was told.

"OK, when are you coming?" he replied.

"Oh, we aren't coming," came the response.

So now, what was the football team going to do? The coaches had to figure out how to transport a traveling party of more than eighty some seventy miles. They called VIP Sports, the bus company who serves them in Abilene, to see if they had any suggestions. We started checking for fifteen-passenger vans, which wasn't much of an option since we found only one available. The coaches even called the Madison school district to see if they could rent several "yellow dog" buses. School district rules, however, said they couldn't go out of state and the team was staying in Iowa.

Just then another charter flight landed at the airport and four buses were there to meet the plane. It was the New Mexico State football team that was flying in to play the University of Wisconsin. The HSU coaches ran down the tarmac and explained their dilemma.

Fortunately, the Madison bus company was cooperative. They said they would take the New Mexico State team to the motel and then come back to pick up the Hardin-Simmons team. They would take them to Platteville and Dubuque and stay with them for the weekend.

It all worked out, and the Cowboys won the game. But it was an example of all the moving parts and what could go wrong when transporting a large group like a football team.

Amazingly, it happens every weekend with college teams and professional teams flying from one end of the country to the other. Most of the time, it works flawlessly.

Favorite Quotes

Let's be honest: In fifty-plus years of covering sports and doing thousands of interviews, there are very few quotes that stand the test of time. There are those few, however, that were humorous or surprising that made them memorable.

Here are a few and the background surrounding the quotes:

In 1989 when the Dallas Cowboys were suffering through their 1-15 year in their first season under the Jerry Jones-Jimmy Johnson era, Buddy Ryan's Philadelphia Eagles sacked rookie quarterback Troy Aikman an NFL record 14 times.

In the Cowboys' locker room after the game, a group of us reporters were standing around all-pro offensive lineman Nate Newton, who was always good for a quote.

"Tough day?" one of the reporters finally asked Nate.

"It was like Pearl Harbor," Newton said. *"They were coming from everywhere."*

Everyone recognizes Kansas City Chiefs quarterback Patrick Mahomes as the top quarterback and perhaps the most exciting player in the National Football League. But when Mahomes was at Texas Tech, he was just the latest in a long line of quarterbacks who put up amazing passing yards in Tech's Air Raid offense.

A relatively unheralded high school quarterback out of Whitehouse in East Texas, Mahomes started just four games as a freshman. But as a sophomore in 2015, he threw for 4,658 yards and 36 touchdowns. Those are incredible numbers, but to put his sophomore season in perspective, consider this: His 4,658 yards were only the sixth most in school history behind B.J. Symons (2003), Graham Harrell (2007 and 2008), Kliff Kingsbury (2002) and Sonny Cumbie (2004). He finished his first full season as a starter with more yards and yards per attempt than Harrell, Kingsbury, Seth Doege and Taylor Potts did in their first years.

Mahomes also rushed for 456 yards and 10 touchdowns as a sophomore, breaking the school record for most rushing yards and touchdowns in a season by quarterback.

It was Mahomes' ability to scramble that separated him from all of the other Texas Tech greats that preceded him over the previous 15 years, according to Kingsbury, who by then was the Red Raiders' head coach.

"He can extend plays as well as I've seen," Kingsbury told me in a story I wrote for *Red Raider Sports* magazine. *"And his accuracy when plays break down, as far as a thrower, moving around, throwing*

from different angles, Pat is the best I've ever been around."

I remember thinking at the time that that was hyperbole from Kingsbury. But after three Super Bowl victories and numerous awards, Kingsbury, who is now the offensive coordinator for the Washington Commanders, was right: Mahomes can extend plays better than anyone I have seen.

———

I had the pleasure of getting to play golf with the legendary Sam Baugh, the former Washington Redskins quarterback who was in the inaugural class of the Pro Football Hall of Fame. Baugh lived on his Double Mountain Ranch in between Rotan and Aspermont in a sparse section of West Texas and in later years only left the ranch to go into town at nearby Rotan or play golf with friends in Hamlin or Snyder.

Former Snyder and Western Texas College golf coach Bob O'Day, who was often Baugh's playing partner, got me the opportunity play a round of golf with him and Baugh at the Western Texas College course in Snyder that now bears Baugh's name. O'Day also organized a fund-raising golf tournament for the scholarship program at Sul Ross State University.

The tournament attracted a number of sports celebrities who came to honor Baugh. One year it was played in Colorado City. The next year it was in Snyder. I got several friends in Abilene to join my team. Our celebrity partner one year was Red Cashion, the long-time NFL referee who had the legendary

"First Down" call. Every time we made a birdie, we had to yell "First Down." Unfortunately, we didn't make enough of them to win the tournament.

The next year our playing partner was Dick Nolan, the former San Francisco 49ers head coach who had been a teammate of Tom Landry's with the New York Giants in the 1950s. Nolan had an unusually deformed wrist. It was almost U-shaped where the wrist connected to his hand.

Finally, someone asked Nolan about it. He explained the biggest difference in the NFL today from when he played was sports medicine.

"I broke my wrist in Detroit in a game against the Lions," Nolan explained. *"We took the train back to New York and they didn't set it until we got back home. The Giants' team doctor was a family friend of the Mara family (which owned the Giants). He was a gynecologist, and the only thing he carried in his medicine bag was a bottle of Scotch."*

———

Hall of Fame quarterback Peyton Manning was not only a great quarterback but he is also a student of the history of the game.

In 2000, two of the National Football League's greatest quarterbacks from different eras got a chance to meet for the first and only time. *Sports Illustrated* in its annual football preview edition paired the up and coming stars at each position with one of the greats of the game at their respective position.

So they paired Manning with Baugh, who was eighty-six at the time. He was one of the greatest two-way players in NFL history. In fact, in 1943 he led the league in passing, punting and interceptions. He still holds the NFL single-season punting record and even all these years later has his name on a number of Washington Redskins' (now Commanders) passing records.

Manning, along with a *Sports Illustrated* photographer, came to Baugh's Double Mountain Ranch. O'Day from Snyder, Texas, was there that day.

"Peyton and Sam sat and talked for about two hours," the late O'Day recalled. "After that, Peyton would call Sam occasionally to talk to him. Sam thought a lot of him, what a nice young man he was."

In 2007, after the Indianapolis Colts won the Super Bowl, Peyton's dad Archie Manning sent a Colts' Super Bowl cap to Baugh, who by that time was living in a nursing home in Jayton, Texas.

Sam and I had talked about that meeting with Manning during the several conversations we had over the years. But it wasn't until Manning came to Abilene to speak at charity event that I learned the interesting way in which Manning got to the Double Mountain Ranch.

Manning and the *Sports Illustrated* photographer flew into Snyder and then planned to make the fifty-mile drive to Baugh's ranch. There wasn't a van to rent in Snyder, however, that was big enough to hold the camera equipment, so O'Day got a local funeral home to lend their hearse to make the drive to the Double Mountain Ranch.

But Manning was quick to point out, *"I certainly didn't ride in the back."*

———

The only time I ever covered spring training, I was in Haines City, Florida, to watch the Kansas City Royals play the St. Louis Cardinals. Royals' outfielder Bo Jackson may be the most amazing athlete to play both football and baseball, starring at running back for the Oakland Raiders and a power-hitting outfielder for the Royals.

I asked Bo for an interview.

"Bo is having a quiet spring," he replied, speaking of himself in third person.

That may not sound like much of a quote, but the next week I read in *Sports Illustrated* that Jackson was declining all interviews that spring. Guess what? I thought I was as good as *Sports Illustrated*. Bo didn't talk to either one of us.

———

One of the most amazing football games I ever covered was a Class 3A high school contest between Abilene Wylie and No. 6-ranked Ballinger. Ballinger's Bearcats led 26-0 at the end of the first quarter, and the game appeared to be total rout. Wylie's

Mike Chapman returned a kickoff 80 yards for a touchdown with 15 seconds left before halftime, but Ballinger still held a 34-14 lead at halftime.

The Bearcats led 41-21 going into the fourth quarter, but Wylie rallied. Chapman, who scored four touchdowns and kicked six extra points, reached the end zone on a 1-yard dive with 55 seconds remaining and then booted the PAT to give Wylie the improbable 42-41 win.

Following the game, I asked Wylie coach Hugh Sandifer what he told his team?

"I told the kids at halftime if they wanted to be involved in the greatest comeback ever in Wylie High School history, they had the opportunity," he said. *"I've seen things like this on TV, but this is the greatest comeback I've ever been involved in."*

My next-door neighbor told me later that he had left the game at halftime. When he picked up the paper the next morning, he thought I must have lost my mind. There was no way Wylie won that game. But the Bulldogs did.

———

The late Spike Dykes was one of the funniest coaches I ever had the pleasure to get to know. Dykes, who was from Ballinger, Texas, got his coaching start in a number of small West Texas schools such as Eastland, Coahoma, Big Spring and Midland Lee before getting into college coaching and eventually becoming the head coach at Texas Tech.

I was in Austin when Dykes' Red Raiders upset the University of Texas. A reporter asked Dykes in the locker room after the game if that was the biggest win of his career.

"Oh, I don't know," Dykes quipped. *"When Coahoma beat Aspermont, that was a pretty big win."*

———

I had the honor to co-write Emory Bellard's autobiography *Wishbone Wisdom* that chronicled the remarkable life of the high school and college football coach who invented the wishbone offense.

I spent hours with Coach Bellard over a couple of years, taping interviews with him. Bellard, who won Texas high school state championships at Breckenridge and San Angelo Central, explained that he had been working on what he called the "triple option offense" for several years. Even at age 80, Coach Bellard was still drawing plays on graph paper.

In the summer of 1968 after he was named offensive coordinator for Darrell Royal at the University of Texas, Bellard explained he brought Coach Royal down on the turf at Memorial Stadium. Using a few seniors who had used up their eligibility but were still on campus during the summer, Bellard played quarterback and demonstrated how the offense, that later became known as the "wishbone," would work. In fact, Bellard said he broke a finger taking a snap during the demonstration.

After the demonstration, Royal gave Bellard his blessing to install the new offense.

"How did that work out?" I asked.

"We lost the first game," Bellard replied, *"tied the next one and then won the next thirty."*

Over half of the national championships between 1969 and 1980 were won by teams running Bellard's wishbone offense.

———

In September 2011, then Texas A&M athletic director Bill Byrne came to Abilene to speak to the local Abilene A&M Club meeting. I was invited to attend and had the opportunity to do a one-on-one interview for my radio talk show.

The college conference landscape was starting to change, so I asked Byrne when we would see the end to all the shuffling of conference alignments.

"Never," he replied.

Of course, he was right, but he didn't let me in on a "little" secret. The very next week, Texas A&M made the surprising announcement that it was leaving the Big 12 for the Southeastern Conference, effective July 1, 2012. I could have had the biggest breaking story of the year. Instead, I could only wish my interview with Byrne had come a week later – or he wasn't as good at keeping a secret.

———

It is always exciting when you have the opportunity to do a one-on-one interview with someone who was the very best at his profession. I had that opportunity when legendary UCLA basketball coach John Wooden came to Abilene Christian University to give a talk on his "Pyramid of Success."

Wooden was 90 years old at the time, but he was still sharp as a tack. His UCLA teams won ten national championships in a twelve-year period from 1964 to 1975, including seven in a row. We talked about those championship teams that included Kareem Abdul-Jabbar and Bill Walton.

When we finished our interview, I told Coach Wooden that my high school basketball team ran a 2-2-1 full-court press because his teams did.

With a smile and twinkle in his eye, Wooden replied, *"A lot of teams did."*

A local TV reporter, who met Wooden after our interview, said, "You are looking good, Coach," to which Wooden replied, *"You either have bad eyesight or you are a damn liar."*

Wooden, known as the Wizard of Westwood, died in 2010 at the age of ninety-nine.

————

Former New York Yankee second baseman Bobby Richardson was a guest on my radio show a couple of times. The Yankees in 1961 – the year Roger Maris hit sixty-one home runs and Mickey Mantle fifty-four – clubbed 225 home runs, which held as the Major League record for thirty-five years.

"I contributed three of those," Richardson laughed.

Although Richardson hit only thirty-four home runs in his career, he hit some dramatic home runs, none bigger than Game 3 of the 1960 World Series. He hit a grand slam and later a two-run single, giving him a World Series record of six RBI in that game.

The Pittsburgh Pirates beat the Yankees in seven games in the 1960 Series, but Richardson, an eight-time all-star, was named the Most Valuable Player, the only player on the losing team to be honored as the World Series MVP.

———

This is the only quote that I didn't hear first-hand, but it is still one of my favorites. It was told to me by the late Gerald Coppedge, who was the boys basketball coach at Abilene High.

Andrae Patterson, a six-foot, nine-inch junior at Abilene Cooper High School, was a *Parade* all-American and the most highly recruited basketball player to ever come out of Abilene. He was being recruited by all the big-name coaches in the country in 1993. Indiana's Bob Knight, North Carolina's Dean Smith and Duke's Mike Krzyzewski, among others, all made their way to Abilene to try to lure Patterson to their programs.

Steve Fisher, who had led Michigan's Fab Five to the Final Four that year, flew into Abilene, and when he got his rental car at the airport, he got directions to Cooper High School.

Only problem was, the rental car attendant at the Abilene Regional Airport gave him directions to Abilene High instead of Cooper. Fisher had done his homework and knew Cooper's coach was Jack Aldridge. When Fisher walked into Eagle Gym, all the players (it was actually a junior varsity practice at the time) stopped, and Fisher walked up to Coppedge and introduced himself.

"Jack, I'm Steve Fisher," he said, shaking hands with Coppedge.

"Nice to meet you, Coach," Coppedge replied. *"But I'm not Jack, and you're in the wrong gym."*

———

In 1988, Hardin-Simmons University in Abilene was a member of NCAA Division I and was playing in the far-flung, short-lived Trans America Athletic Conference that included three schools in Texas, one in Arkansas, one in Louisiana, one in Alabama, three in Georgia and one in Florida.

Stetson University in Deland, Florida, was the host for the men's conference basketball tournament, which was held in the new convention center in nearby Daytona Beach.

Arkansas-Little Rock was the defending tournament champion, having upset Notre Dame in the first round of the NCAA Tournament a year earlier. And the Trojans were heavily favored to win it again.

My hotel for the tournament happened to be right on the

beach in Daytona, and MTV had set up its headquarters there to broadcast the spring break frivolities. Trust me, there were plenty beer-drinking college kids and girls in bikinis in our hotel.

The University of Texas-San Antonio team was staying in the same hotel that I was in, while UALR coach Mike Newell kept his team in Orlando and bused an hour into Daytona Beach each day for the tournament.

Well, lo and behold, UTSA upset Arkansas-Little Rock in the championship game to earn the school's first-ever bid to the NCAA Tournament.

In the post-game press conference, I asked the always colorful Texas-San Antonio coach Ken Burmeister about his strategy of staying right in the middle of Spring Break Headquarters, while Arkansas-Little Rock stayed in Orlando to avoid the party atmosphere.

"We didn't judge any wet T-shirt contests," Burmeister replied, *"but we didn't miss many, either."*

Right Place, Right Time

The 1980s were the glory years for golf in Abilene, Texas. Fairway Oaks Golf and Racquet Club was built and for ten years Abilene was host to a PGA Tour event. For me, it was the unique opportunity to do one-on-one interviews with some the great names in golf, players like Gary Player, Payne Stewart and Hal Sutton, just to name a few.

I even got to play in a pro-am tournament with Don January.

Not coincidentally, the 1980s were also the hey-day for high school and junior golf in Abilene as both Abilene Cooper and Abilene Wylie won numerous high school state tournaments. The best of those young golfers was Bob Estes, who led Cooper to three consecutive Class 5A state championships in 1982-84.

Estes then went to the University of Texas where he was an all-American and was named the recipient of the Nicklaus Award as the nation's top collegiate golfer as a senior. He earned his PGA Tour card on his first try, thus beginning a long, successful career as a professional golfer.

Estes didn't earn the first PGA Tour title until 1994, however. I was in College Station to cover the Texas A&M-Baylor football game in the fall of 1994. When I called in my story to the *Abilene Reporter-News*, the copy desk told me that Estes was leading the Texas Open in San Antonio going into Sunday's final round.

"We ought to cover that," they said.

"You are right," I responded. "Wonder how I can get a pass?"

There were only a handful of reporters still left in the pressbox, but one of them was Kevin O'Keefe, a sports writer from San Antonio.

"Hey, Kevin, any chance you have the phone number for the press room at the Texas Open?" I asked.

Amazingly, he did. Even though it was getting dark and Saturday's tournament round was over, someone answered when I called the press room. I explained I was from Abilene and wanted to cover the final round of the tournament. He said he would have a pass waiting for me.

This was before GPS or the internet, so I didn't know the best way to get from College Station to San Antonio – or how long of a drive it was. I didn't know where the golf course was located. And I didn't even know what time Estes would tee off.

My wife had gone with me to College Station. She had left from work and was in heels, so we had to stop to buy her some tennis shoes so she could walk the golf course.

Somehow, we found the golf course. I got my pass and took my laptop to the press room. We then walked out to discover Estes was just preparing to tee off at No. 1. So we got to walk all eighteen holes with his parents Tommy and Bobbie Estes as we watched Bob capture his first PGA Tour tournament championship and receive a check for $250,000. It was the first of four wins Estes had on the PGA Tour, and he is still playing in the PGA Champions Tour.

What a thrill to be able to be there to cover a local athlete claim his first PGA Tour win. Right place, right time.

———

That was just the first time that circumstances had allowed me to write a story about Estes. But it wasn't the last.

Five years later in 1999, I was invited to attend the Gutenberg Awards dinner at Abilene Christian University where the school's journalism department honors its outstanding alumni. One of the honorees that year was Doug Ferguson, the long-time golf writer for the Associated Press. We were seated together at the dinner and had a great visit getting to know each other.

A few weeks later, Payne Stewart was killed in a tragic plane crash, just months after he had won the U.S. Open.

The next week was the season-ending PGA Tour Championship in Houston, and the biggest story, of course, was Stewart. The PGA had flown the players to the funeral earlier in the week and a special tribute was held for Stewart prior to Thursday's opening round. I remember watching on TV as a person playing the bagpipes walked away from the first tee and into the dense fog.

Ferguson, of course, was filing stories for the Associated Press about the tribute as well as the tournament itself. One of the first stories he filed that morning had one line near the bottom of the story which mentioned that Estes, as a tribute to Stewart, had hit a putt off the first tee the same distance as Stewart's winning putt on the final hole at the U.S. Open.

His later stories never mentioned Estes' putt, so I called good friend Denne Freeman, the long-time Texas sports editor of the Associated Press in the Dallas.

"I know it is asking a lot, but is there any chance you could get a hold of Doug Ferguson and see if he could send me a short story about Estes' tribute putt that we could run in the *Reporter-News?*" I asked.

Freeman said he would try and an hour or so later called back to say Doug would do that for me.

Ferguson sent us a nice sidebar story with a quote from Estes that we were able to run in the paper as a localized sidebar to the biggest national sports story of the day.

Like being able to be at the Texas Open in San Antonio or having dinner with Ferguson just weeks earlier, it seemed like fate had allowed me to be in the right place at the right time.

Golf Coverage

The late Bob Green, who was the long-time golf writer for the Associated Press before Doug Ferguson, once spoke to a civic club meeting in Abilene, Texas, and he was asked about his own golf game.

"I don't play golf," he responded.

"You don't play golf!," was the incredulous response from the questioner in the audience. "You travel to the great golf courses in the world – Augusta National, Pebble Beach and St. Andrews – and you don't play golf?"

"When I started with the Associated Press," Green replied, "I covered murder trials. You don't have to do what you write about."

I do play golf, although not very well and lately not that often. But much of my career has involved covering golf in one form or another.

During my five years working in radio at KWCK/KSER

Radio in Searcy, Arkansas, we broadcast a golf tournament live. Searcy Country Club was host to the annual K.B. Rand Memorial Golf Tournament, one of the larger amateur tournaments in the state

We broadcast all fifty-four holes of the tournament. Not just reporting scores. We had mobile units and followed the leaders, reporting each shot of the tournament just like television. Now broadcasting golf on the radio may sound crazy, but it was really pretty neat and made the tournament something special.

The K.B. Rand tournament was the first time I saw future PGA champion John Daly, who was just coming off his freshman year at the University of Arkansas at the time. Daly amazed the gallery with his long drives.

On the last day of the tournament, Daly, who grew up in Dardanelle, Arkansas, and one of the state's best amateur golfers Wyn Norwood (who later became the golf coach at Arkansas-Little Rock) were tied for the lead. Daly probably drank a beer a hole on that hot steamy Sunday afternoon and lost the tournament to Norwood. Obviously, Daly's bad boy reputation as a free spirit began long before his tumultuous professional career.

———

When I moved to Abilene, Texas, in the fall of 1986, one of the first events I got to cover was the Gatlin Brothers Southwest Classic, a PGA Tour event and eventually a Senior

Tour tournament that was held in Abilene.

The pro golfers loved to come to Abilene near the end of the season because they got to go dove hunting in addition to competing for a $400,000 purse. The Abilene tournament attracted all of the top golfers of that era with the exception of Jack Nicklaus and Arnold Palmer.

I got to do interesting one-on-one interviews with Gary Player, Hal Sutton, Payne Stewart, Mark Calcavecchia, Paul Azinger, Lee Trevino, George Archer and Bruce Crampton, just to name a few. I called the tournament a "touch of big-time" that came to Abilene for a week each fall.

———

Because of the close relationship between the Colonial Invitational golf tournament in Fort Worth and the Gatlin Brothers Southwest Classic in Abilene, I got to play in the Colonial Wide-Open, a media scramble held several weeks before the Colonial PGA event, for about ten years.

I was even on the second-place team in 2002 and have a beautiful crystal bowl to prove it. But trust me, I didn't have much to do with our team's performance. Each media team was paired with a Colonial committee member. It just so happened, my team's committee member that year was the defending Colonial club champion.

———

In 1991, my publisher, who was a golfer, suggested I play the golf courses in the Big Country and write about them. What a sweet deal. Over the next two years, I played twenty-two courses in the area, ranging from the challenging Cliffs course at Possum Kingdom Lake to the pecan-tree-lined San Saba Country Club, as well as Abilene Country Club, Fairway Oaks Country Club, Dyess Air Force Base's Mesquite Grove Golf Club, Diamondback Golf Club and Maxwell Municipal Golf Course in Abilene.

Most of my rounds of golf were at small-town nine-hole courses in the area. It turned out to be extremely popular. Golf pros, the best players in those small towns and sometimes even the mayors in those communities joined me for my golf game. I even got to play 18 holes with legendary former NFL quarterback Sam Baugh at the Western Texas College course in Snyder that bears his name.

———

I also started writing a weekly golf column, promoting those small-town tournaments, charity events and telling of holes in one or other interesting golf stories.

Two of my favorites involved unusual holes-in-one.

Hoolie White of Anson made two holes-in-one in his life and they were on the same hole —more than fifty years apart. White had been playing the nine-hole Anson Golf Club regularly since 1938. He said he couldn't remember whether Franklin Roosevelt or Harry Truman was president when he made his first hole-in-one. It was in the 1940s, but he was not sure what year and there is no record of it.

Bill Clinton was president when White made his second hole-in-one on the same par-three, 139-yard sixth hole on April 28, 1997.

It just so happened that the same day White made his hole-in-one, I was playing in the Colonial Wide Open at Colonial Country Club in Fort Worth. One of my playing partners was John Lumpkin, the Dallas bureau chief for the Associated Press.

A couple of weeks later, Lumpkin was in Abilene, and stopped by my office to talk golf. I told him the story of White's hole-in-one and gave him a copy of my column. He sent it to AP staff writer Mark Babineck in Lubbock. Babineck went to Anson and wrote a feature on White. Don Cronin from *USA Today* then called me for some additional information. He had seen the AP story on White and was writing a story of his own about the hole-in-one for that national publication.

White died a little more than two years later at age ninety-three. The number six hole at Anson Golf Club has been renamed "Hoolie's Hole," and the club's annual "Sponsors' Classic" golf tournament held each October was renamed the "Hoolie" in memory of White

The other unusual hole-in-one story came in the Lee Medical Supply Charity Golf Classic, benefitting Hospice of Abilene, at Abilene Country Club. Fred Lee Hughes, a second generation car dealer and the former mayor of Abilene, said his company, Fred Hughes Motors, had offered a new car for a hole-in-one in charity tournaments for years but had never given one away.

On June 24, 1994, Hughes Motors had a new Buick LeSabre as the prize for a hole-in-one at the par-three, 179-yard tenth hole. I was playing in the tournament and was on the fourth tee box when tournament officials came racing over in a golf cart to find me.

"Someone just made a hole-in-one and won the car," they said excitedly.

"Who was it?" I asked.

"Fred Lee Hughes," they replied. That's right, Hughes used a seven-wood to make a hole-in-one to win his own car.

Five days later, Paul Harvey included the story of Hughes' hole-in-one on his nationally syndicated radio show.

"Fred Lee Hughes of Abilene, Texas, donated a Buick LeSabre for a hole-in-one," Harvey announced, "and then he won it."

And that was the rest of the story.

Olympians
I Have Known

Track and field Olympians often provide some of the most interesting stories. Not only do they have to be the best in the world to win a gold medal, but they also have to be the best in the world at the time of the Olympics.

Since the Olympics happen only once every four years, sometimes it doesn't work out. The best in the world might be injured or not at their best at the right time.

Here are the unique stories of the six Olympians I got to know, several of whom became good friends.

Glenn Cunningham was a legend in Kansas, growing up in the small southwestern Kansas town of Elkhart. As a native Kansan, I heard of Cunningham all my life, but I never met him until I moved to Arkansas.

I actually ran in track against his son Glenn Cunningham

Jr. in high school. The elder Cunningham placed fourth in the 1,500 meters in the 1932 Olympics in Los Angeles and won a silver medal in the 1,500 in 1936 in Berlin, the Olympics best remembered for Jesse Owens' four gold medals while competing in front of Adolph Hitler.

After his running career was over, Cunningham and his wife ran the Glenn Cunningham Youth Ranch in Leon, Kansas, helping 10,000 needy and abused children.

Sometime in the late 1970s, Cunningham moved his youth ranch to Conway, Arkansas. That is when I got acquainted with Cunningham and invited him to speak to my Rotary Club in Searcy. The older Rotarians were thrilled to meet Cunningham because they remembered the inspirational story of his life. In fact, several remembered reading comic books as youngsters that told of Cunningham's remarkable career.

If you don't know the story, you will be amazed. When Cunningham was eight years old, his legs were very badly burned in an explosion caused by his brother accidentally putting gasoline instead of kerosene in the can at his school. His brother Floyd, 13, died in the fire. When doctors recommended amputating his legs, Cunningham was so distressed his parents wouldn't allow it. The doctors predicted he might never walk normally again.

He had lost all the flesh on his knees and shins and all the toes on his left foot. His transverse arch was practically destroyed. However, his great determination, coupled with hours upon hours of a new type of therapy, enabled him to gradually regain the ability to walk and to proceed to run.

It was in the early summer of 1919, when he first tried to walk again, roughly two years after the accident. Imagine that: thirteen years after he walked for the first time he ran in the Olympics.

In 1934, Cunningham set the world record for the mile run at 4:06.8, a mark which stood for three years. He also set world records in the 800 meters in 1936 and the indoor mile in 1938. His personal best time in the mile run was 4:04.4 at Dartmouth College's indoor track. That time was never accepted as a world record, however, because Dartmouth had provided Cunningham pacing runners, which was against the rules at the time.

It would be twenty more years after Cunningham set the world record, that England's Roger Bannister finally became the first to break the four-minute mile, running 3:59.4 in 1954.

I remember Cunningham telling me that breaking the four-minute mile was never a goal of his. He simply ran to win. He claimed he could have broken the four-minute barrier. He was also worried about the strength of his legs that had been so badly burned in his youth, so he started slow, running in the pack. He would be fresher in the second half of the race and would almost be sprinting the last 100 yards to the finish

Although he was the greatest miler of his era, he failed to win a gold medal in the Olympics. But his remarkable story inspired others for years to come.

———

Billy Olson grew up in Abilene, winning a state championship in the pole vault in 1978 at Abilene High School. He stayed at home in college at Abilene Christian University where he competed under the tutelage of ACU coach Don Hood, considered one of the top vault coaches in the world.

Olson won a NAIA national championship every year in college and was considered a leading contender to win a gold medal in the event at the 1980 Olympics in Moscow. The vaulter to beat in 1980 was Poland's Wladyslaw Kozakiewicz, and Olson had beaten him in a meet in Stockholm, Sweden before the Olympics.

That intriguing matchup never happened, however, as President Jimmy Carter decided the USA would boycott the 1980 Games in protest of the Soviet Union's invasion of Afghanistan.

For the next several years, Olson and Sergei Bubka of the Soviet Union waged a dual as the two top pole vaulters in the world, competing in meets that drew huge crowds and national television audiences. Olson was the first vaulter to clear nineteen feet indoors and the first American over that height. In 1986, he soared a career-best 19 feet, 5-1/2 inches at an indoor meet in East Rutherford, N.J. He set eleven world records, the first coming in 1982, his senior season at ACU.

The 1984 Olympics in Los Angeles would be Olson's chance at redemption. But he injured his foot in the first outdoor meet of the season and was unable to compete in the Olympics. Bubka wasn't in LA, either, because the Soviets boycotted the games in retaliation to the USA boycott four years earlier.

Olson qualified for the 1988 Olympics in Seoul, South Korea, but by that time he was past his prime and placed 12th in his specialty. Bubka, who competed for Ukraine after the Soviet Union broke up, won the gold in 1988.

Olson and I became friends shortly after I moved to Abilene. We actually played golf together a few times. His daughter Madi won a pair of state golf championships at Abilene Wylie High School.

A political decision, an injury and eventual aging prevented one of the world's top pole vaulters from ever winning an Olympic medal.

———

Bobby Morrow and Billy Olson had two things in common – both were Olympians and both competed for Abilene Christian University. But that is where the similarities end.

While timing was never right for Olson in the Olympics, Morrow made the most of his one and only Olympic experience. Morrow won gold in the 100, 200 and 4x100 relay in the 1956 Olympics in Melbourne, Australia, in the greatest performance by an American sprinter since Jesse Owens in 1936 in Berlin.

Morrow grew up in San Benito in the Rio Grande Valley and returned to his hometown as a relatively reclusive farmer after his track career was over. While Olson and I were friends, I met Morrow only once when he came back to ACU to speak at a chapel. I even got to hold one of his Olympic gold medals.

Before I moved to Abilene, the only thing I knew about the Key City was that Bobby Morrow ran track at Abilene Christian. He adorned the cover of *Sports Illustrated* as well as *Sport* and *Look* magazines as the star of the 1956 Olympics. It is not an overstatement to say Morrow put Abilene Christian on the national map.

———

One of my favorite events to cover was the University Interscholastic League state track and field championships in Austin, Texas. It was an exhausting but exciting three days covering the top track athletes from the Big Country compete against the best athletes from around the state.

Of all the outstanding performances I wrote about in fifteen years of covering the state track meet, the top performances certainly belonged to Abilene High's Jonathan Johnson in 2001, the last year I covered the state championships.

Johnson shattered the state's longest standing record when he won the Class 5A 800-meter run in 1:48.21, eclipsing the old mark of 1:49.20 that had stood for thirty-four years. His time was the seventh fastest 800 ever run in the Unites States by a high school halfmiler.

As amazing as his run was in the 800, it wasn't his top performance of the 2001 meet. In the final race of the night – and Abilene High needing at least a second place in the 1,600-meter relay to claim the Class 5A boys' team title – Johnson outdid his own performance of slightly more than an hour earlier.

The Eagles were in third place when Johnson got the baton from teammate Robert Spells for the anchor lead. Johnson was nearly twenty yards behind Houston Washington's anchor man James Bell.

Johnson caught Bell on the final curve and the two headed down the homestretch at Mike Myers Stadium stride for stride. Abilene High's relay team of Tyree Gailes, Shawon Harris, Spells and Johnson was clocked 3:11.69. Houston Washington was right behind at 3:11.72.

As I made my way down to the track to interview Johnson, the first person I ran into was Texas Tech track coach Wes Kittley, who had earlier signed Johnson to a letter-of-intent to run track for the Red Raiders.

"Good recruiting job, Coach," I told a beaming Kittley.

"This is the greatest day of my career," an exhausted Johnson told me. "I wanted the (800) record and the mile relay wanted to win. It was a great day."

It wouldn't be the last great day for Johnson, however. Just three years later, as a college junior, Johnson won the 800 at the U.S. Olympic Trials to qualify for the Olympics in Athens,

Greece.

When Johnson won the Olympic Trials, he flashed the Texas Tech "Guns Up" as he cross the finish line. There was a story behind that.

"He was so tight before the race," Kittley recalled. "I told him I would meet him at the finish line, and you give them the 'Guns Up' when you win. He kind of smiled and it kind of broke the edge with him. After the race, I asked him how in the world did you remember to do that?"

"Coach, it was the last thing you told me," Johnson said with a laugh.

Johnson made it to the semifinals in the 800 in the 2004 Olympics in Athens, Greece, before he suffered dehydration and failed to qualify for the finals.

Still, it was quite a feat to think here was a kid I had covered playing high school football and running track, and only three years later he was running with the best in the world in the Olympics.

Johnson earned sixteen all-Big 12 honors and nine all-American awards during his four years at Texas Tech. He won three consecutive Big 12 titles and two NCAA championships in the 800.

———

Dean Smith and I met for lunch one day at a restaurant in downtown Abilene.

"Dean, I was watching the movie Eldorado on TV last night," I told Smith. "Were you in it?"

"You didn't see me?" Smith replied. "I got stabbed in a poker game right at the start of the movie."

I became acquainted with Smith when we inducted him into the Big Country Athletic Hall of Fame. He was already a member of the University of Texas Hall of Fame, the Texas Sports Hall of Fame, the Texas Cowboy Hall of Fame and the Hollywood Stuntman Hall of Fame. We occasionally met for lunch whenever he was in town.

Smith grew up on a ranch between Breckenridge and Graham, some seventy-five miles northeast of Abilene, Texas. He wrote a book "From Olympic Gold to the Silver Screen" about his remarkable life shortly before his death at the age of ninety-one in 2023. Smith, who was still living on the ranch at the time of his death, was one of the most interesting people I have ever met.

Before his movie career, he was an Olympic gold medalist. He was a sophomore at the University of Texas when he qualified for the 1952 Olympics in Helsinki, Finland. Smith placed fourth in the 100-meter dash in the closest finish in Olympic history. The top four runners were all timed in 10.4, but Smith was picked fourth, costing him a medal.

But he later earned a gold medal when he ran on USA's winning 4x100 relay team.

Smith came back to Texas after the Olympics, played

football for the Longhorns and was drafted by the Los Angeles Rams. When the Rams traded him to the Pittsburgh Steelers during training camp, he decided to give up football and try to fulfill his dream to be in the movies.

Smith had made an acquaintance with Oklahoma native and budding actor James Bumgarner a couple of years earlier when he was running the Coliseum Relays in Los Angeles. When Smith was cut by the Rams, he went to the Hollywood studio to look up Bumgarner and get his help in getting into the movies. The movie studio, however, told him they didn't know anyone by that name.

So Smith returned home to Texas. But one day he was reading the *Dallas Morning News* and read a story about a new play opening in Dallas starring James Garner. Bumgarner had changed his name to Garner. So Smith went to Dallas to meet Garner, and that friendship helped him get into the movies. His athletic ability and the fact that he had grown up riding horses made him a perfect candidate for the golden era of Westerns.

Smith appeared in ten John Wayne movies as well as dozens of other movies and television shows. In my favorite John Wayne film "McClintock," Wayne is chasing Maureen O'Hara when she jumps out of a second story window into a haystack. That was actually Smith wearing a dress and a wig.

It is one of many memorable moments in Smith's career as an actor and stuntman. The Big Country Athletic Hall of Fame in the Mall of Abilene has not only the cleats on display that he wore in Helsinki but also a collage of pictures of all the famous actors he appeared with during his lengthy Hollywood career. His was a most remarkable life.

———

Jim Ryun was the greatest middle distance runner in American history. Growing up in Kansas in the late 1960s, Ryun was the biggest story in the Sunflower State. Not Kansas State or KU basketball or the Kansas City Chiefs could compare to Ryun, who was the subject of many stories and books. Local television stations even broadcast his races live.

My first cross country meet as a freshman in high school in 1967 was at the Wamego Invitational, one of the state's largest high school cross country meets in Wamego, Kansas. As we lined up to start the race at the Wamego Country Club, they announced on the PA system that the course record for the two-mile course was 9:18, held by Jim Ryun of Wichita East.

I turned to the runner standing next to me and laughed, "Well, that record is safe today."

Ryun and I discussed running at Wamego and our memories of growing up in Kansas in the 1960s when I met him for the first time several years ago. Mark Miller of the Edward Jones investment firm brought Ryun into Abilene, Texas, to speak to a seminar and invited me to come meet him. It was a chance to meet my childhood hero.

Ryun's accomplishments are amazing. He was the first high

school runner to break the four-minute mile. In fact, he did it five times in high school, including at the Kansas state high school meet. He made the Olympic team in the 1,500 meters as a high school junior in 1964, the second youngest American male track athlete to ever qualify for the Olympics. A year later, he won the 1965 AAU Championship race in a time of 3:55.3, beating Olympic gold medalist and former world record holder Peter Snell. That high school record stood for thirty-six years.

Al with Olympic miler Jim Ryun.

In 1966, at age nineteen, Ryun set world records in the half-mile (1:44.9) and the mile (3:51.3). In 1967, Ryun broke his own world record in a time of 3:51.1, a standard that stood for almost eight years.

Ryun was the overwhelming favorite to win the gold in the 1968 Olympics. But running in the high altitude of Mexico

City, Ryun finished runner-up to Kip Keino of Kenya, who ran an incredible race, setting an Olympic record of 3:34.91 in the 1,500, a mark that held for sixteen years.

Ryun made one last try at the Olympics in 1972 in Munich, Germany, but he was tripped and fell down in a preliminary heat of the 1,500. Although the International Olympic Committee acknowledged that a foul had occurred, the U.S. appeal to have Ryun reinstated in the competition was denied by the IOC.

The greatest middle distance runner of that era has only one silver medal to show for his three Olympic appearances, proof that timing is sometimes everything when it comes to the Olympics. Ryun later served an eastern Kansas district in Congress for ten years.

Field of Dreams

"This field, this game, is a part of our past. It reminds us of all that was good and that could be good again. Oh, people will come, Ray. People will most definitely come."

That, of course, is a famous line delivered by James Earl Jones in the movie "Field of Dreams."

I am one of those who came. In 1997, my wife and I flew to Omaha, picked up my mother-in-law and sister-in-law and drove to Wisconsin for a relative's high school graduation. On the way home, I made a take a detour to Dyersville, Iowa, so I could visit the movie site where one of my all-time favorite movies was filmed.

I ended up with much more than just a trip to the baseball field in the middle of a cornfield. I ended up with one of my favorite columns, as reprinted here from the *Abilene Reporter-News*:

No one can believe how prophetic that line was when Terrance Mann (played by James Earl Jones) told Ray Kinsella (played by Kevin Costner) that people would come to see the baseball field that a voice had instructed him to build out of cornfield on his farm in the popular 1989 movie "Field of Dreams."

Certainly not screen writer Phil Alden Robinson, who first took an interest in the novel *Shoeless Joe* written by Canadian author W.P. Kinsella in 1982.

Robinson recognized the potential of the heartwarming story and found himself with his film crew in the cornfields of Iowa during the summer of 1988. But it is doubtful he anticipated what has happened since making the movie, which was nominated for Best Picture in 1989.

And certainly not this baseball fan, who made a twenty-five-mile detour during a recent vacation trip to Iowa and Wisconsin just to see the site where the movie was made.

And most certainly not Paul Scherrman, who grew up Farley, just five-minute drive from the Field of Dreams.

"It's unbelievable," Scherrman said. "I was out there last week, and they just keep on coming. I never thought it would be this popular."

Keith Rahe, who managed one of the souvenir stands at the Field of Dreams movie site, said it is estimated that 50,000 to 60,000 people visit Dyersville each year just to see the field.

Producers considered sites in 20 different states, as well as several Canadian provinces, before choosing the cornfield, which is actually on two farms, owned by Don Lansing and Al and Rita Arneskamp, three miles from the small community of

Dyersville.

Dyersville is located 25 miles west of Dubuque, which sits on the Mississippi River dividing Iowa and Wisconsin in northeast Iowa.

Robinson, during the early months of 1988, was reportedly approaching the Lansing farm from behind a hill. When it came into view, he shouted "That's it! That's my farm."

How little did he realize the impact of his statement.

Lansing's farm house was renovated, with the wrap-around porch added to accommodate the porch swing. The interior of the house was also remodeled to give it an open, airy feeling. All of the scenes in the house and on the porch were filmed there. It remains today exactly as it was after Universal Studios made the renovations in 1988.

It is a three-mile drive on a narrow paved road northeast out of Dyersville – through cornfields, of course – to get to the movie site (there are signs to direct you). For one who has probably watched the movie a dozen times, it was almost breathtaking to come around the corner and see the field and house, exactly as it was in the movie.

The only thing different today from when the movie was filmed in1988 is the two souvenir stands. There is no admission charge to visit the site, and fans can go on the field to play catch or run the bases.

When filming was completed on August 16, 1988, the land owners assumed it was all over.

In fact, the first year after the movie the outfield was plowed up and corn planted.

But people kept coming.

"It would have never dreamed what has happened," Scherrman said. "But a couple of years later, the owners realized what they had. And the outfield was put back. The field today is exactly like it was in the movie, the same dimensions."

Scherrman, who played professional baseball in the Washington Senators' and Texas Rangers' organization in 1971 and '72, is the catcher in the baseball scenes on the field.

"They put out an ad in the Dubuque paper for people with baseball experience," Scherrman said. "I gave them my baseball resume. But I lied about one thing – my age. I think they were looking for players in their 30s."

He is forty-eight now.

But Scherrman made the cut from nearly 200 who tried out. The team then held practices under the direction of Baltimore Orioles coach Don Buford, father of Rangers centerfielder Damon Buford, and former Southern California baseball coach Ron Dedeaux.

After that, Scherrman and the Ghost Players (who came out of the cornfields to play on the field which Ray Kinsella had built) spent twenty-two days on the film set.

So how many minutes was Scherrman in the movie?

"You mean how many seconds, not minutes," he said, laughing. "There are only two or three shots that I'm in. It's less than a minute."

Scherrman's biggest scene is when Kinsella's brother-in-law walks across the field, oblivious to the Ghost Players who are playing on the field.

"I'm the catcher who grabs the batter when he takes off after him," Scherrman said. "We were on the set twelve hours a day. It was very tedious. But it turned out glamorous."

Glamorous, indeed.

Scherrman, who is a state representative in Iowa and a third-generation owner of the family farm implement business, still plays baseball. In fact, when his schedule allows it, he still plays for the Ghost Players, an organization when has evolved from the popularity of the movie.

"I made a three-week trip to Japan last year with the Ghost Players," he said. "We put on Little League clinics, a comedy routine or play competion in both baseball and softball."

The Ghost Players, who have been to Japan, Cuba and all over the United States, do corporate outings and appear at minor league parks and other celebrity outings.

In fact, the Ghost Players, who wore old Chicago White Sox uniforms in the movie, made their third annual appearance Saturday night at Chicago's Comiskey Park.

Next weekend, they return for their annual three-day appearance in Chisholm, Minnesota, hometown of Archer "Moonlight" Graham, played by Burt Lancaster in the movie.

Graham had the shortest stint major league history – one game with no at-bats – before becoming a doctor for forty-eight years in Chisholm. His story is an integral part of the movie plot.

"Baseball has been very good to me," Scherrman said. "Just signing a pro contract was a dream come true. And then doing the movie, going to Japan with the Ghost Players and people like you calling for interviews, I've been very fortunate."

But no one could have foreseen a baseball field cut out of cornfield becoming the region's top tourist attraction.

Next time you are looking for a movie to watch, check out "Field of Dreams" and watch it again. Maybe then you'll see why Terrance Mann said the field "reminds us of all that was good and could be good again."

You will see why a lifelong baseball fan took a twenty-five-mile detour off his designated route to the see the field.

And you will understand why a baseball field in the middle of an Iowa cornfield continues to draw nearly 60,000 people annually to a town of 4,000.

"It's unbelievable," Scherrman said. "They just keep on coming."

A Missed Scoop

One of the things I liked most about being a sports reporter was getting the "scoop," breaking a story before any of the competition. It doesn't happen often, but it is gratifying when it does.

This, however, is a story of my biggest missed scoop.

In 1998, Hardin-Simmons University was a member of NCAA Division I and played in the 10-team Trans America Athletic Conference that stretched from Texas to Florida. The men's conference basketball tournament that year was hosted by Stetson University in Deland, Florida, at the new convention center in nearby Daytona Beach.

The Cowboys had had a good year and thought they had a shot at earning the tournament's automatic bid to the NCAA Tournament. So I talked the *Abilene Reporter-News* management in letting me go Daytona Beach to not only cover the tournament but also stay a couple of extra days to write some feature stories from spring training.

The Texas Rangers trained in those days in Port Charlotte, which was a long way from Daytona Beach and Orlando, where

I flew into. So I scheduled myself to cover two Houston Astros games in nearby Kissimmee and one Kansas City Royals game in Haines City.

My first game on Sunday after the Saturday TAAC tournament championship game was an Astros game against the Pittsburgh Pirates. When I arrived at the game, I found that Pam Postema was the home-plate umpire that day. She was a Triple-A umpire in the Pacific Coast League and was trying to become the first female umpire in Major League Baseball.

I thought that would make a good story.

The game occurred with no controversy and Postema had a good, consistent strike zone.

When I went the locker room after the game, I asked Houston manager Hal Lanier about Postema's performance.

"I thought she did a good job," Lanier said.

I then talked to Charlie Kerfeld, who had pitched in relief for Houston that day. Oddly enough, a few years later Kerfeld became an acquaintance when he managed the Prairie Dogs minor league baseball team in Abilene.

"She is a good umpire," Kerfeld said of Postema. "She called our games when I was in Tucson in the Pacific Coast League last year."

So I seemingly had no story other than just a mention that Postema had been the home-plate umpire. But imagine my surprise when I picked up the Orlando paper the next morning and read a story about what Bob Knepper had said. Knepper was the starting pitcher that day for the Astros, and he was quoted as saying women shouldn't be umpires or President of the United States. I hadn't bothered to talk to Knepper after the game.

That became the biggest sports story in the nation and set off such a furor that the National Organization of Women (NOW) picketed all of the Astros' home games that season. And I had missed the story. Postema never landed a Major League umpiring job, and it was thirty-seven more years until Jen Pawol became the first woman to umpire in a Major League regular-season game in August of 2025.

If it is any consolation, however, the story I wrote was a feature on a rookie catcher who was trying to make the Astros' roster. He had hit a double and a home run that day.

His name? Craig Biggio. Of course, Biggio went on to collect more than 3,000 hits – all with the Astros – and has been elected to the Baseball Hall of Fame in Cooperstown. Maybe I missed the scoop, but I found it satisfying that I chose a pretty good player to feature.

Old-Timers Interviews

One of my favorite things to cover that most people don't even know about was the Old-Timers baseball games – not the games itself but the media availability.

In the late 1980s and 1990s, The Equitable sponsored Old-Timers games at various Major League ballparks. Former Fort Worth Cats manager and long-time Texas Rangers executive Bobby Bragan always hosted the event in Arlington.

The former big leaguers would have a golf outing on the Friday morning before the Saturday night baseball game. Then on Friday afternoon, they would be available for interviews with the media. Not many media attended each year, but it was always a thrill for me.

As a long-time baseball fan, I got to sit down and do lengthy one-on-one interviews with Bob Gibson, Brooks Robinson, Bobby Richardson, Leo Durocher, Enos Slaughter and Johnny Mize, just to name a few. All provided wonderful stories for interesting columns and features.

One year I even interviewed David Clyde, who was going to pitch the next night in the Old-Timers game and, oddly enough, was younger than Nolan Ryan who was the starting pitcher for the Rangers that night.

You may remember that the Rangers drafted David Clyde right out of high school in Houston in 1973. Just two weeks after he pitched in the state high school tournament, he was the starting and winning pitcher for the Rangers in the first sellout in franchise history since moving to Texas a year earlier.

Clyde's career flamed out and he became a shining example of how NOT to handle a high school signee and how NOT to bring them up to the Major Leagues too early. Clyde may have been ready for the majors physically, but not mentally for all the pressure and lifestyle changes that came with it.

He was very nice and upfront, however, in talking about what he went through in his brief career.

The late Bob Tiffany, who had been an executive with The Equitable in New York City before retiring and moving back to his wife's hometown of Abilene, was emcee for the dinner that night. He invited me to be his guest at his table at the dinner, where I got to sit next to former St. Louis Cardinals outfielder Lou Brock and enjoy chatting baseball with him that evening.

My favorite story from the Old-Timers media events, however, took me back to my childhood. I was an avid baseball card collector as a kid, and I had a 1959 card of Milwaukee Braves pitcher Lew Burdette.

The photo on the card showed Burdette pitching left-handed, but every baseball fan knew Burdette was right-handed.

I even read an article once that noted the 1959 baseball card of Burdette was considered a collector's item but wasn't worth much money because so many cards had been printed. I had always wondered how that happened.

Well, Burdette was standing at the bar, so I went up to him to ask how the card came out with him pitching left-handed. Burdette explained that TOPPS always took the pictures for the baseball cards at the start of spring training, and Warren Spahn, who was the greatest left-handed pitcher of that era, told Burdette, "Let's fool them. I'll borrow your glove and I will pitch right-handed and you pitch left-handed."

Burdette said the TOPPS folks realized their mistake and came back at the end of spring training to re-shoot Spahn's picture. But they never caught the error in Burdette's photo, so the 1959 card of the right-handed Burdette had him pitching left-handed.

While Burdette and I were talking, former Major League umpire Len Roberts, who was going to be umpiring the Old-Timers game the next night, and eighty-eight-year-old Hall of Fame umpire Jocko Conlan joined in the conversation.

Just then Mark "The Bird" Fidrych walked in, with his long, lanky gait and his trademark curly hair hanging over his ears and on his back collar. Fidrych was wearing a baseball cap, faded blue jeans with a bag stuffed in his back pocket, and a purple shirt with white polka-dots that looked like something one would have seen at Haight-Ashbury in San Francisco in 1969.

You'll remember that the colorful Fidrych took the baseball world by storm in 1976 as a rookie with the Detroit Tigers. He was the American League Rookie of the Year, posting a 2.34 earned run average and led the AL that year with 24 complete games. He would talk to the baseball and would get down on his knees to pat the mound with his hands. Fidrych became the most popular and colorful storyline of the 1976 season.

Unfortunately, injuries cut short his career and he was never able to duplicate his remarkable rookie season.

"Who is that?" Conlan asked.

"That's the 'The Bird,' Mark Fidrych," Burdette replied.

"He was a helluva pitcher," Roberts added.

"And he was good for the game," Burdette said.

Conlan took another look at Fidrych and asked, "Does he own a comb?"

I still laugh as I remember that story. Conlan umpired in the Major Leagues from 1941-65, but obviously Fidrych represented a new generation of "Old-Timers" that he hadn't encountered before. Time marches on.

Major League Baseball, in an effort to modernize its game, experimented in spring training in 2025 with a rule change in which a batter can challenge the ball or strike call by the umpire, and the ruling is either upheld or reversed by an automated system.

For several years MLB has used a system in which the manager can challenge an out or safe call at the plate or on the bases, or a hit that is ruled fair or foul. If the call is challenged, the umpires put on the headset and wait for a ruling from New York where MLB has a variety of camera angles to view to either uphold or reverse the call. The idea of the rule changes, of course, is to get the call right.

But it has taken away some of the colorful part of baseball when a manager goes out to argue a call, going nose-to-nose in a heated exchange with the umpire. Who can forget fiery managers like Earl Weaver or Billy Martin arguing with the umpire's decision? I even remember Lou Piniella kicking dirt on the umpire's shoes.

It may not be the look that baseball wants, but it is certainly part of baseball's colorful past. I was reminded of an interview I did one year at the Old-Timers media day with the always controversial manager Leo Durocher, who was well into his 80s at the time.

Durocher, who managed the New York Giants and Brooklyn Dodgers, was holding court the Old-Timers media event in Arlington when he told this story:

"One of my players hit a ball down the right-field line," Durocher recalled. "When the ball hit the line, chalk flew up (signifying a fair ball), but the first-base umpire signaled foul ball. So I went running out to argue, and the fans were yelling, 'Give 'em hell, Leo.'"

"When I got out there, the first-base umpire said, 'I'm sorry, Leo. I blew the call, but there nothing I can do about it now.' So what was I going to do? I had my reputation to uphold.

"So I stuck my finger in the umpire's chest and said, 'Where are we going to dinner tonight? I bought last night, so you are buying tonight.' And then I walked back to the dugout, and all the fans were cheering and yelling, 'Attaboy, Leo.'"

Somehow, whether right or wrong, that seems more entertaining than the manager sitting in the dugout putting his hands over his ears to signal to the umpire that he wants to challenge the call. Not sure Leo Durocher could have managed in today's baseball era.

A Fourth Out and Unusual Plays

I am a big fan of unusual plays, something we have never seen before, or plays that test our knowledge of the rules. I have often written about such plays.

It has been more than forty-five years since I witnessed perhaps the most unusual baseball play I have ever seen, but I remember it like it was yesterday. I have eagerly awaited seeing it happen again so I could impress everyone with my knowledge of the rule. But, alas, I have never seen it occur again. And probably never will.

It was a Sunday afternoon American Legion baseball game in Searcy, Arkansas, between Searcy and Batesville. Although I broadcast many of the Legion games there for several years, I wasn't calling the game at Berryhill Park in Searcy that day. Instead, I was sitting in the dugout, keeping the scorebook.

Here was the situation:

Batesville had runners on first and third base with one out. The Batesville batter hit a bloop fly down the right-field line that looked like it was going to fall in for a base hit. Searcy's right-fielder, who was probably the fastest player on the team, made a tremendous diving catch for the second out of the inning.

As he rolled over and got back to his feet after the diving grab, he was probably only thirty or forty feet behind first base and he realized the runner on first base, thinking the ball was going to fall in for a hit, had taken off for second. Now, the runner was scrambling to try to get back to first base.

Searcy's right-fielder threw the ball to the first baseman to easily get the force for the third and final out of the inning.

In the meantime, the home plate umpire signaled the runner coming in from third had touched home plate before the putout was made at first base, so the run counted.

Searcy manager Steve Smith, however, came out to argue that the runner had not tagged up at third base, so he wanted to appeal that the runner had left the base too early.

"You can't appeal," the umpire said. "There are already three outs."

Searcy lost the argument and the run counted that day. Somehow, that didn't seem right to me, however. I asked a number of local umpires about the play, and all said they weren't sure of the rule.

After much searching, I discovered the baseball rule book does take into account just such a play. The team in the field can stay on the field and appeal for a mythical fourth out if it potentially takes a run off the board.

Searcy could have stayed on the field and made an appeal throw to third base. If the umpire determined the runner had indeed left the bag too soon, the run would not have counted.

If that would have happened, I am not sure how I would have marked it in the scorebook, but a legal fourth out remains maybe the most unusual play I have ever seen.

A play similar to that reportedly happened in a 2023 game between the Cleveland Guardians and Minnesota Twins, but no one knew the rule so no appeal was made. With replay and challenges in Major League Baseball today, the play will probably never happen again. But if it does, I know the rule.

———

If you think you have seen everything that can happen in a baseball game, hang on because, if you go to enough games, you are surely going to see something else that will test your knowledge of the rules.

This one was passed along to me from a 2025 Western Athletic Conference game between Abilene Christian University and Grand Canyon University at ACU's Crutcher Scott Field.

The Wildcats had a runner on second with one out when Diego Cardenas stepped to the plate. Cardenas hit a deep fly to center field that was aided by the wind (yes, surprise, surprise, the wind was blowing strong in March in Abilene, Texas). The ball kept carrying. The ball hit the top of the centerfielder's glove and caromed over the fence for a home run.

That wasn't the issue, however. Cardenas, thinking the ball was going to stay in the ballpark, was digging around the bases, hoping for a double or maybe a triple. The runner on second held up between second and third, waiting to see if the ball was going to be caught.

Cardenas overran the base runner, thus was called out for passing a runner. After much discussion, Cardenas was ruled out for the second out of the inning but the base runner was awarded home plate.

If you are scoring at home, Cardenas may have hit the ball out of the park but he was only credited with a fielder's choice and a run batted-in. It may be a while before you see that happen again.

Baseball on the Radio

The greatest announcers are the Major League Baseball announcers on the radio. For 162 games a year, they can tell stories, weave endless statistics into the broadcast and paint a picture of the game for the listeners in what could be called "theater of the mind."

The radio announcers provide so much more information than those on TV. For baseball fans of a certain age, radio is how they learned to love the game, long before baseball became a regular staple on television.

Long-time Texas Rangers fans are familiar with the immense talents of Eric Nadel, a Ford Frick winner who has been the Rangers' radio voice since the early days of the franchise. For me, the voice I grew up with was Monte Moore. He was the voice of the Kansas City A's from 1962-1967 and then moved west with the team when the franchise moved to Oakland.

He continued as the principal radio voice for the A's through 1977 and served as its television announcer through 1980. He returned to do the A's television broadcasts from 1988 to 1992 before retiring. Moore also served as the play-by-play voice on

NBC's backup Game of the Week for several years.

Al with baseball broadcaster Monte Moore.

Moore's daughter Deona Shake teaches at Abilene Christian University and when the A's won the 1989 World Series, I interviewed her about her memories as a little girl riding in the A's victory parade with Dick Green and Reggie Jackson following their consecutive World Series titles in 1972, 1973 and 1974.

I told Deona that I grew up listening to her dad.

"If he is ever in town, tell him to give me call," I said.

To my surprise, the phone rang at the office over Christmas vacation. It was like a voice out of my past. It was Monte, and we had a delightful visit, talking about my memories of listening to him on the radio. I told him I learned to keep score while listening to him on the radio.

In fact, I recalled a Saturday afternoon game when Dagaberto "Campy" Campaneris made his Major League debut. I laughed and told him I didn't know how to spell Dagaberto or Campaneris at the time.

Moore then told me the story of Campaneris, who didn't speak any English, and the unusual details of his debut that day. Team officials pinned two notes on his shirt. One said to put him on a flight to Minneapolis. The second note was to be given to the taxi driver when he arrived in Minneapolis to take him to Metropolitan Stadium.

Moore said Campaneris arrived at the ballpark just an hour before the first pitch, and he then homered in his first at-bat, one of only a handful of players to accomplish that feat.

Several years later, in 1996, I came back from lunch and began trying to figure out what I was going to write for my column in the *Abilene Reporter-News* that day. A bulletin then came across the wire telling of the death of former A's owner Charlie Finley.

Moore had been the longest-tenured employee of the controversial Finley. So I called Deona, and she gave me the telephone number of the radio station in Porterville, California, which Moore had bought following his retirement from the A's.

I called the radio station. But it happened to be the Martin Luther King holiday, and Moore was not in the office. I explained who I was and the purpose of my call, and the radio station secretary surprisingly gave me Moore's home number.

I was the first to tell him of Finley's death. We had a great interview, recalling his memories of working for Finley. A month or so later, Moore was in Abilene. He came by to thank me for the interview, noting he had been on two national talk shows that evening to discuss his memories of Finley. But he said I was the first to tell him of Finley's death.

Monte also was my guest in the studio on my radio show several years later, telling baseball stories for an hour. His son Bruce even surprised him by calling into the show from London, England.

Moore's grandson Bryson Shake works at the Big Country Athletic Hall of Fame museum, and Moore, who is now ninety-five, visited the museum recently, allowing me to catch up with him again.

Nadel, St. Louis Cardinals announcer John Rooney and former Kansas City Royals announcer Steve Physioc are all friends, and Nadel and Physioc have all been guests on my radio show over the years. But Monte Moore was the voice I grew up with. How lucky I am to become a friend all these years later.

The broadcasting of each sport has its own rhythm. Baseball is much more laid back, punctuated by moments of exciting action. Basketball is fast-paced, continuous action. Football requires the description of the play and then re-setting the down and distance after each play.

In each sport, you can never give the score too often. In basketball, I give it after every basket because fans in the stands naturally look at the scoreboard following each change of possession. In football and baseball, I try to give the score frequently because you never know who just tuned in, and nothing is more frustrating than listening to a broadcast and not knowing the score for long periods of time.

In college and professional games, statistics are provided. But in high school, you have to keep your own statistics.

Another thing the radio announcer has to do before each game is check the pronunciation of players on both teams. I still distinctly remember a football broadcast I did fifty years ago – my first year of broadcasting – between Hanover and Powhattan, two small towns in northeast Kansas. Hanover is a predominately Bohemian/German settlement, while Powhattan includes the nearby Kickapoo Indian Reservation.

Here was my call in the game that I still remember: "Powhattan has the ball at the forty-yard-line. Albert Whitebird is the quarterback under center. He takes the snap and pitches out to Running Deer for a sweep around right end. Running Deer is tackled behind the line of scrimmage for a loss by Zabortrsky and Zarbyncky. What a great American game!"

———

One final broadcasting note: It was perhaps the most bizarre setting for a broadcast ever. Carder Buick in Searcy, Arkansas, sponsored an AAU men's basketball team for years comprised of former collegiate players.

One year, Carder Buick qualified for the national tournament in St. Augustine, Florida. I went along to broadcast their games. The national tournament was held at the Florida School for the Deaf.

School officials let the students out to watch the afternoon games. So here I was broadcasting a basketball game in a gym full of students with very little noise. The students were all busy communicating with each other by using sign language.

Ultimate Trivia

I hosted "Let's Talk Sports," a live daily sports talk show on the radio on KWKC/KZQQ in Abilene, Texas, from 2003-2020. The hour-long show featured coaches' shows with the three high school and three college football coaches in Abilene, other special guests and mostly call-ins from listeners who just wanted to talk sports.

It was fun because I never knew what the next question or comment from a listener was going to be. I enjoyed the challenge of being able to talk off the cuff on a variety of sports topics. My radio show always included sports trivia, too.

It is easier to find answers to trivia questions today with the internet and sources such as ESPN Stats. But that was not the case some 40-plus years earlier.

This is the story of a several-years-long search for the answer to the "ultimate" trivia question.

My first full-time job after college from 1975-77 was working for KNDY Radio in the small town of Marysville, Kansas, located near the Nebraska border. Besides doing the sports play-by-play and a shift as a country music disc jockey, I also sold advertising. I called on the businesses in all of the small towns east of Marysville.

One of my favorite clients was Lewis Seed & Fertilizer, owned by the father-son team of Jim and Duke Schramm, in Home, Kansas, just a spot in the road a few miles east of Marysville on Highway 36. They were sports fans, and Duke had played on a high school state championship basketball team in Marysville and refereed high school football, so I enjoyed stopping in occasionally just to visit and talk sports.

One day when I stopped by, Duke was sitting at his desk looking at the *Baseball Encyclopedia*, the book that lists the statistics of every player in Major League Baseball history.

"I've got the ultimate trivia question for you," Duke said. "Remember when Bert Campaneris played all nine positions in a game for the Kansas City A's in 1964?"

"Yeah, I think I listened to that game," I replied.

"It says here that Campaneris struck out one batter in his one inning on the mound," Duke continued. "Who was it?"

"I know it was against the California Angels, but I don't remember who he struck out," I stated. "I will see if I can find out."

Well, time passed and I never thought about it. Shortly after that I left Marysville for a job in Pittsburg, Kansas, and then moved to Searcy, Arkansas, to take a radio job. One night I was sitting in my apartment spinning the dial on my radio when I came across a sports talk show on the powerful 50,000-

watt radio station in Cincinnati.

That show was normally hosted by former Bengals tight end Bob Trumpy, but Dick Carlson was hosting the show that night. I had listened to Carlson on the radio in Kansas City when I was growing up in Kansas, but he had moved to Cincinnati to become the play-by-play voice for that city's team in the World Hockey League.

I have hosted radio talk shows for nearly twenty years and have been a guest on numerous shows, but that is the only time I ever called a show like I always asked my listeners to do.

I called shortly before 11 p.m., which was midnight in Cincinnati, so Carlson took my call as the final call of the night before he signed off.

"I have the ultimate trivia question," I said.

"Well, I don't know about that," he responded.

I proceeded to explain to him that I knew he was in Kansas City in 1964 and that was the year that Campy Campaneris played all nine positions in a game for the A's.

"He struck out one batter," I said. "Who was it?"

"I remember that game, but I don't remember who it was," Carlson replied. "Call me back tomorrow and I will have the answer for you."

Well, I have never heard that show again. But several months later, I was skimming through the *Sporting News* and found the Q&A column called "Your Question Please." A reader from Cincinnati asked the question, "Who did Bert Campaneris strike out when he played all nine positions in a game for the Kansas City A's in 1964?"

After several years, a long-distance phone call and a question in a national publication undoubtedly inspired by my late-night phone call, I finally found the answer. It was Bobby Knopp, the second baseman for the California Angels.

I sent this story to Duke Schramm, who I haven't seen in nearly 50 years to let him know I finally found the answer to his "ultimate" trivia question. Better late than never.

From Cuba to Red Raiders to Rangers

I love finding unusual angles when writing feature stories. In 2019, *Red Raider Sports* magazine assigned me to do a feature on Josh Jung, who later that summer became a first-round draft choice of the Texas Rangers and is now the Rangers' starting third baseman.

Here is the feature I wrote on Jung prior to the start of the 2019 spring baseball season at Texas Tech:

What did you do on your summer vacation?

Josh Jung went to Cuba. It wasn't exactly a vacation, but the Red Raiders junior third baseman did become one of only a small number of Americans to visit the isolated island nation last summer.

Jung was selected to the USA Baseball Collegiate National Team, which included the nation's top college freshmen and sophomores. The team swept five games from Chinese Taipei and won three out of five from Japan in games played in Carey, N.C., before traveling to Cuba, where the USA team captured three of four games against the Cuban national team.

"It was an unbelievable experience," Jung said. "It was good to reach that honor, but when I put on the jersey with 'USA' on it in red, white and blue, it really sunk in."

And what was it like visiting Cuba?

"Culture shock," he responded. "It was like a throwback in time with the old cars and weathered buildings. The taxis looked like go-carts. But the food wasn't bad. There was a place right across from our hotel that had great chicken tacos."

Being named to the USA national team is just one of many honors that Jung has received since arriving on the Texas Tech campus two years ago from San Antonio MacArthur High School. He started every game as a freshman, batting .306 with 75 hits, including 14 doubles, two triples and six home runs. He was named the Big 12 Freshman of the Year.

"I wanted to start as a freshman," Jung recalled. "It was a big transition. College baseball is a lot faster. I had to groove my game and learn the strike zone. In high school, I was the dude. I had to accept the fact that I wouldn't be the dude in college and made sure I was getting extra hacks in the cage."

Last year, as a sophomore, Jung started all 65 games again at third base, helping the Red Raiders to a 45-20 record and their third trip to the College World Series in the last five years. He led the Big 12 in batting (.392), hits (103) and RBI (80) on the season, earning five all-American honors. His hit total was third nationally, while his RBI total was fourth.

"I played summer ball in California between my freshman and sophomore seasons," Jung explained. "I learned to handle pitches and be more selective, really sticking to one side of the plate and going back to fundamentals, grooving my swing and driving it gap-to-gap."

Jung said he is comfortable, even if he is down in the count with two strikes.

"I preload my hands, eliminate any movement in my swing and expand the plate one or two inches when I'm down 0-2," he stated. "I spread out and try to battle to eliminate strikeouts. Avoiding strikeouts means you put pressure on your opponent to make a play."

On April 21 last year at New Mexico, Jung completed the sixth cycle in Texas Tech history, going five-for-five with eight RBI, four runs and walk, becoming the first Red Raider to go five-for-five when hitting for the cycle. He had a single, double, triple, two home runs and a walk in his remarkable performance that day.

"Since the time Josh has been here, he has been a guy that continued to work and continue to grow," said Texas Tech head coach Tim Tadlock. "He is a guy that really strives to get better each day. He can handle a ball on both sides of the plate. Obviously, his defense has been outstanding. Really, there isn't a phase in the game he hasn't grown, and I would think he's going to continue to that."

Jung may not have considered himself "the dude" as a freshman, but there is no doubt he is that guy for the Red Raiders now. He has been named a first team preseason all-American by three different publications, and he has been selected the Big 12 preseason player of the year.

The Red Raiders are ranked in the top five in the nation in three different preseason polls, and Jung is a major reason for that.

"This year's team has tons of potential," he said. "We will be faster. That extra tool of running puts pressure on the defense. Offensively, we will be one of the best teams in the country. Our pitching staff has so much potential, too."

There are projections that claim Jung will be a top-10 pick in June's amateur draft, but he said he is not worrying about that now.

"I want to make sure we have a good season," he emphasized. "My focus is geared toward the team. I want to mentor the young guys to learn and grow. I want to bring a national championship back to Lubbock. We have the best chance to do that this year. If I do that, the draft will take care of itself."

Surprising West Texas

Whether writing a feature story or doing a radio talk show interview, I love surprises. It doesn't happen often, but it is fun when the interviewee reveals an unusual story that I had never heard before.

There is no better example of a surprising interview than one I did with the commissioner of Major League Baseball.

I only covered a handful of Texas Rangers' games during my fifteen years as sports editor of the *Abilene Reporter-News*. But I always tried to go to Opening Day.

It was Opening Day 1990. A group headed up by George W. Bush had bought the Rangers a year earlier. Bush's father, then President George H.W. Bush, was scheduled to throw out the ceremonial first pitch.

I always tried to go early so I could be on the field during batting practice. I might pick up a story idea or two, but mostly it was just to soak up the atmosphere.

As I walked on to the field at old Arlington Stadium that day, I noticed a group of reporters gathered around a golf cart sitting in front of the first-base dugout, so I walked over to see who it was that was drawing their attention. It was Fay Vincent, the baseball commissioner.

Pretty soon, the group wandered away, leaving just me and the commissioner, so I introduced myself.

"Where are you from?" Vincent asked me.

"Abilene," I replied.

"Ah, Abilene," he responded. "West Texas."

"What do you know about West Texas?" I responded. The minute I said it, I thought it sounded like a rather smart-aleck comment. But, since Vincent was from Connecticut, graduated from Yale and now worked in New York City, I thought it was a legitimate question.

"Ever heard of Andrews or No Trees?" Vincent asked.

"I have been to Andrews," I said. "I have heard of No Trees, but I have never been there."

Vincent proceeded to tell me a story about his experience in West Texas. He said his best friend growing up was Bucky Bush, George H.W. Bush's younger brother. The summer after he and Bucky graduated from high school and before they entered college at Yale, they came to West Texas to work as roughnecks in the oil field for the elder Bush.

"I'll never forget the last day that summer before we were headed back to college, George called us into his office in Midland," Vincent said. "He said 'Hold out your hands. It looks like it was a good summer. No one lost a finger (a hazard for those working on an oil rig).'"

Vincent, the eighth commissioner in Major League Baseball history, died in early 2025 at the age of 86. The stories about his career talked about him making sure the 1989 World Series took place after the San Francisco earthquake and his regrets about being unable to get the owners and players to reach a labor settlement, a conflict that cost him his job and ultimately resulted in the extended baseball strike of 1994.

No stories about Vincent's career, however, mentioned the commissioner of baseball working in the oil fields in the Permian Basin of West Texas. I guess the story was my exclusive, a pleasant surprise of an interview that day.

Walk-Offs

Wonder when the term "walk-off" became part of our sports vocabulary?

When Bill Mazeroski hit a home run off New York Yankees pitcher Ralph Terry in the bottom of the ninth inning in Game Seven of the 1960 World Series to give the Pittsburgh Pirates a 10-9 win and the Series championship, it was just described as the game-winning hit.

Sometime over the past twenty or so years, however, game-winning hits like Mazeroski's home run have become known as "walk-offs."

The term, of course, is an accurate description. Because of the base hit or home run, a field goal or touchdown, or a basket, everyone walks off, thus the term "walk-off." The game-winning play occurred to end the game with, in the case of football or basketball, meaning time had expired.

I have certainly seen dozens of "walk-offs" over the past fifty years, and no play is more exciting – or heartbreaking – than a "walk-off." There is no doubt, however, what is my favorite "walk-off," simply for a purely personal reason.

My grandson Jaxon Hansen was a good enough baseball player at Abilene Wylie High School to be a four-year starter at shortstop or third base, earning honorable mention Class 5A all-state honors and playing two years of junior college baseball at Angelina College in Lufkin.

In the 2018-19 school year, Wylie was making the jump from Class 4A to Class 5A, which some believe may be biggest adjustment for schools changing classifications. Wylie's football team had gone 0-10 that fall after being a traditional state-wide power in Class 4A.

The Bulldogs' baseball team, however, made the postseason in the spring of 2019 and was facing Lubbock Cooper in a best-of-three bi-district playoff series. The two teams split the first two games of the series, and the third and deciding game went to extra innings tied 3-3.

Lubbock Cooper scored a run in the top of the eighth to take a 4-3 lead. Wylie had runners on second and third with two outs in the bottom of the eighth, when Jaxon, who was a sophomore at the time, came up to bat. He fell behind in the count at no balls and two strikes. On the next pitch, however, he ripped a double into the gap in left field, scoring the two runs and giving Wylie the "walk-off" series win.

By that time, I had given up my high school broadcasting duties to just sit the stands and be a cheering grandpa. But a friend, sitting in the press box, videotaped the "walk-off" and subsequent celebration on his cell phone, including the excited call by Wylie's radio broadcaster Matthew McGraw who was going crazy, and sent it to me.

I still have the video on my phone, and every so often I will watch it just to remember the excitement of the moment. I have never regretted giving up high school broadcasting to be able to watch my grandkids on the football or baseball field or the volleyball court. I wouldn't trade those years for anything.

But no doubt the "walk-off" in that baseball playoff game in 2019 remains the top highlight. It is the thing that dreams are made of, and certainly dreams of a proud grandpa and grandma.

Grandson Jaxon Hansen being interviewed after his walk-off hit in 2019 bi-district series.

Women's Basketball

It seems like many in the sports world discovered the excitement of women's basketball for the first time in 2024 with the remarkable long-range shooting and passing ability of University of Iowa guard Caitlin Clark. She broke the NCAA scoring record (for men and women) in leading the Hawkeyes to back-to-back NCAA national championship games.

Clark was then the first pick in the WNBA Draft by the Indiana Fever and drew record crowds – and record TV ratings – wherever she and the Fever went. She was named the WNBA Rookie of the Year. What she did for women's basketball is nothing short of amazing.

Women's basketball, however, played an important role in the start of my career.

In 1974, I was a junior radio-TV major at Kansas State University. I was learning my craft on the all-volunteer 10-watt student radio station KSDB-FM, and we had broadcast a few women's basketball games since no one else was carrying them. By contrast, K-State men's basketball had a state-wide radio network.

K-State was chosen to be the host site for the week-long national tournament of the Association of Intercollegiate Athletics for Women (AIAW). It would be eight more years before the NCAA would take over governance of college women's basketball, and all schools – no matter what size – were competing in the same national AIAW tournament in 1974.

Several of us aspiring sports broadcasters devised a plan to offer our broadcast services of the tournament games to the hometown radio stations free of charge. I ended up broadcasting games that week to Queens, New York; Salt Lake City, and Jackson, Mississippi, among other cities.

The national championship game featured Immaculata College, a tiny Catholic all-girls school in Pennsylvania, against Mississippi College, which is now an NCAA Division II school in Clinton, Mississippi, just outside of Jackson.

Immaculata, known as the "Mighty Macs," captured its third straight AIAW national championship that night with a win over Mississippi College. Immaculata, coached by Cathy Rush, is considered the birthplace of modern women's college basketball.

Two of the stars on that Immaculata team went on to outstanding coaching careers of their own. Theresa Shank Grentz, who is a member of the Naismith Memorial Basketball Hall of Fame, won 681 games as the coach at Saint Joseph's, Rutgers, Lafayette and the University of Illinois. Marianne Crawford Stanley, the point guard on that Immaculata team, was the head coach at Old Dominion, the University of Pennsylvania, the University of Southern California and the University of California. She later was the head coach of the Washington Mystics in the WNBA.

It was a memorable week for someone who had dreamed of someday broadcasting college basketball.

So imagine my surprise some 30 years later when I was in Clinton, Mississippi, to broadcast the Hardin-Simmons University game in the American Southwest Conference men's basketball tournament. As I was killing time before the start of my game, I found a shadow box in the lobby of the Mississippi College gym highlighting the Lady Choctaws' AIAW national runner-up team.

I had broadcast their championship game so many years earlier. I told that story to the school's sports information director, who introduced me to a faculty member who was keeping the scorebook at the tournament. He told me he had been a student at Mississippi College and was a member of a boys team that practiced against the girls team that year.

Sometimes it is small world.

———

The next year, as a senior at Kansas State, I got my first paying job broadcasting games for a new FM radio station in Marysville, Kansas, a town of 3,500 some 50 miles north of Manhattan near the Nebraska border. I did a game-of-the-week

IT MUST BE A BIG GAME

during football season, and broadcast Marysville High School basketball games that winter. When it came time for postseason basketball tournaments, I broadcast games of the smaller area towns.

One of those small towns was Centralia, Kansas, which is best known as the hometown of former NFL running back John Riggins. Centralia had an outstanding girls basketball team that year, and I was able to broadcast my first state championship as Centralia captured the Class A state title with a win over Medicine Lodge in the title game.

It was just the third year that the Kansas High School Activities Association had held a state tournament for girls basketball and that year decided to also have a two-year experiment it called "Grand State" in which it would bring the four state champions to Topeka for tournament a week after the state tournaments.

Centralia won the Class 2A state championship and then made it to the Grand State championship game against Wichita South. Centralia, with only about 500 people in the whole town, would take on Wichita South, which had more than 2,000 students.

It turned out to be a terrific game, which Wichita South won 68-64. Centralia was actually a better team than Wichita South except for one sophomore on the Wichita South squad. She was amazing. She would rebound on one end, take the ball to the other end herself and then score. She was bigger, stronger and faster than everyone else on the court. She finished with 36 points that night. I had never seen a girl with that kind of ability on the basketball court.

Her name? Lynette Woodard. She later became the all-time leading scorer in AIAW history at the University of Kansas and the first woman to play for the Harlem Globetrotters. Her collegiate scoring record held until Caitlin Clark broke it in 2024.

I "discovered" Woodard as a high school sophomore in 1975.

———

Covering women's basketball continued to be an important part in both my newspaper and radio career, including broadcasting the Hardin-Simmons Cowgirls' trip to the NCAA Division III Final Four in Springfield, Massachusetts, in 2006.

When I first left the *Abilene Reporter-News*, I had plenty of opportunities to cover high school playoff games for the *Dallas Morning News, Fort Worth Star Telegram, Lubbock Avalanche Journal, Amarillo Globe News, Midland Telegram, Odessa American* and *San Angelo Standard Times* on a freelance basis.

Newspapers, however, have eliminated those freelance opportunities as they apparently no longer want a written story of games involving their area teams. In some cases, independent web sites, such as Big Country Preps in Abilene and Hub City Preps in Lubbock, have picked up that slack.

Good friend Randy Rosetta hired me to cover a girls Class 5A Division II regional semifinal playoff game in 2025 involving Lubbock Monterey and Fort Worth Brewer for Hub City Preps. It was the rare opportunity to see the nation's top recruit, senior guard Aaliyah Chavez of Monterey.

Interviewing the nation's number one high school girl basketball player, Lubbock Monterrey's Aaliyah Chavez, in 2025.

The five-foot-eleven-inch five-star guard didn't disappoint, scoring fifty points in leading Monterey to a 76-40 romp over Fort Worth Brewer. It was a performance that received national attention on ESPN and in *Sports Illustrated*, one of nine times she topped fifty points in a game during her high school career.

Because of Abilene's geographical location, Lubbock Monterey played four playoff games in Abilene en route to winning the 2025 state championship. Having the opportunity to see the nation's top girls basketball player drew huge non-partisan crowds from Abilene and all across the area in addition to the Monterey faithful, crowds that were previously unheard-of to watch girls basketball. How often does one get to see the number one ranked player in the nation?

Chavez averaged 34.9 points, 9.1 rebounds, 4.3 assists and 3.7 steals per game as a senior and finished her high school career with 4,796 points, 1,200 rebounds and more than 700 assists. Amazingly, she scored more than 1,000 points in each of her four high school seasons at Monterey and was named the 2025 Naismith High School Player of the Year, the 2025 Gatorade National High School Player of the year and the two-time Texas Gatorade Player of the Year. She was also named to the McDonald's High School All-American team.

When she announced her commitment following the season to play basketball at the University of Oklahoma, ESPN carried the ceremony live. Not sure if I have ever seen that before.

Chavez is the closest thing to Caitlin Clark I have ever seen in high school, and what a thrill it was to see the nation's top high school player in action in person several times during the 2025 playoffs.

Crazy Buzzer Beaters

We have all seen basketball games decided on a shot at the buzzer. But I broadcast a game that was certainly the most unusual last-second finish I have ever seen.

It was 1979 and I was broadcasting a men's basketball game between Harding University and Arkansas College (now known as Lyon College) in Batesville, Arkansas. The Arkansas College gymnasium is similar to many high school gyms – bleachers on each side with scoreboards on the wall behind each basket at the end of the court.

My broadcast seat was at midcourt at the top of the bleachers behind the scorer's bench.

Arkansas College led by one point when Harding's Kenny Moorer sank two free throws with seven seconds remaining to put the Bisons up by one point.

The Scots then raced down court and fired up an 18-footer from the left wing. The ball hit the heel of the rim and bounced straight up in the air. An Arkansas College player leaped high above everyone else, grabbed the ball above the rim and then dropped it back in the basket. When he did, the scoreboard behind the basket read 0:00.

The crowd in the packed gym was roaring and I couldn't hear the buzzer. But my gut instinct was the Arkansas College player didn't release the follow shot prior to time expiring. That was my initial call on the broadcast.

To my surprise, veteran Arkansas basketball official J.W. Fullerton, who was the out official in the two-man officiating crew with the same angle to the basket and scoreboard that I had, turned to the scorer's bench with his palms upturned and a shrug of his shoulders, signifying he, too, couldn't tell whether the shot should count. I have never seen an official do that before or since.

So the decision was left in the hands of the score clock operator, who was probably an Arkansas College faculty member. He said the basket was good, which set off quite an argument, as you might expect. I did a lengthy postgame commentary, before taking my end-of-the game commercial break, describing normally mild-mannered Harding coach Jess Bucy vociferously arguing at the scorer's bench. All, of course, was to no avail.

Coach Bucy sent the tape of the game's finish to the scoreboard manufacturer, who claimed there is a milli-second difference between the buzzer and clock going to 0:00. The manufacturer even admitted it couldn't tell whether the basket should have counted.

This was before a red light was put behind the backboard

to help make those last-second calls easier to determine. In fact, it was just a year or two later that the red light behind the backboard became mandatory. I have often wondered if that Harding-Arkansas College game had some bearing on the rule change requiring a red light behind the backboard.

———

Of course, technology continues to change. Now, there is a monitor courtside at the scorer's table at college games which officials can use to decide timing issues, out-of-bounds calls, flagrant fouls, time remaining on the clock, or whether a shot should be a two-pointer or a three-pointer.

In 2024, for the first time, I would see the officials announce to the television broadcasters what they are looking for when they go to the monitor, and then, after a decision is rendered, they come back to announce what the call was.

In broadcasting NCAA Division III basketball, we now have the use of the courtside monitor in the American Southwest Conference, but the officials never come over to announce what they are looking for or what the decision was. It often leaves me guessing on my broadcast.

But even the use of a courtside monitor has been an evolution.

Nearly 20 years after the crazy Harding-Arkansas College finish, rivals Hardin-Simmons and Mary Hardin-Baylor were playing a men's basketball game at the Mabee Complex in

Abilene, Texas. Mary Hardin-Baylor hit a shot that would have tied the game, but it was ruled to be released after the buzzer and thus didn't count, giving Hardin-Simmons the win.

But that was only part of the story. Here is the column I wrote following the last-second HSU-UMHB finish as reprinted from the *Abilene Reporter-News:*

Just thirty-five days after the controversial finish to the Texas Tech-Texas A&M men's basketball game in Lubbock, we almost had an instant replay Saturday in Abilene.

Saturday's game could have been the first test of a new rule that was passed following the Red Raiders' game against the Aggies – but it wasn't.

Instead, Hardin-Simmons University's 79-77 win over Mary Hardin-Baylor turned out to be just a thrilling finish. But it could have been a lot more.

First, a little background;

A&M's Andy Leatherman hit a last-second shot on Jan. 15 at the new United Spirit Arena in Lubbock to give the Aggies an 88-86 victory over Texas Tech, undoubtedly the most controversial play of the college basketball season because of the way it was handled.

The officials huddled, called the basket good, then reversed their decision and called it no good before changing their minds again and giving the Aggies the victory. The A&M team left the floor, got on the bus and headed for the airport, while Texas

Tech players and fans remained in the arena for nearly an hour before learning they had definitely lost the game.

After that game, the NCAA Men's and Women's Basketball Rules Committees met and made a rare rule change in the middle of the season, allowing instant replay to be used to determine whether or not to allow a last-second game-determining field goal.

Ron Holmes, the head men's basketball coach at McMurry University, is the Division III representative on that rules committee.

"What sold me on it was the point that (University of Kansas coach) Roy Williams made," Holmes said. "He said we have correctable errors to fix things in games. Why wouldn't you want the outcome at the end of a game – that is the most important thing – to be correctable?"

Holmes said that to his knowledge the new rule has not been used since it was implemented on Jan. 28.

It could have been Saturday afternoon at HSU's Mabee Complex. Or could it?

That is apparently an unresolved issue at this point.

Mary Hardin-Baylor had the ball out-of-bounds at midcourt with 4.32 seconds left, trailing 79-77. The Crusaders got the ball to Sherrard Taylor, whose running jumper from the right side of the lane missed. But Jason Winn, MHB's six-foot, eight-inch post, tipped it back in – simultaneously with the final horn sounding.

The outside official — the one facing the basket on the opposite side of the scorer's bench who had the call in that situation — immediately and decisively waved the basket off, saying Winn's tip did not precede the final horn.

The officials immediately ran off the court with Mary Hardin-Baylor coach Kent DeWeese in hot pursuit. Obviously, DeWeese believed it should have counted.

Hardin-Simmons coach Dennis Harp said he has watched the videotape of the play over and over.

"I thought at the time it was no good, but, of course, I was wanting it to be no good," Harp said. "After watching the replay, it was unbelievably close. But it looked to me like the horn sounded a fraction of a second before the ball left his hand."

Harp said HSU's video of the play is not definitive because the clock — and the red light behind the backboard that is supposed to go off at the same time as the buzzer — can't be seen in the video. The horn, however, can be heard distinctively on the video, but Harp said when he stops the video at the precise moment, it kills the audio portion of the tape.

The three officials who worked the game came into Harp's office after they had showered Saturday and asked to watch the video. After watching the tape, they believed they had made the right call — the ball was still touching Winn's hands when the buzzer sounded.

But could Mary Hardin-Baylor have appealed the decision and forced the officials to look at the replay immediately before determining whether or not the basket should have been disallowed.

Holmes said yes.

"You don't have to have a monitor on the table at courtside," said Holmes. 'We discussed that at our meeting because most Division III schools don't have courtside monitors."

Holmes said that if DeWeese had appealed the call, the officials could have gone to HSU's video camera, which was set up atop the bleachers in the Mabee Complex.

But Tony Stigliano, the coordinator of officials for the Great Southwest Officials Association that assigns officials for the American Southwest Conference, has a memo on his Web site, dated Jan. 26, for the officials about the new rule that gives an opposite interpretation.

According to Stigliano's memo, "Pending further interpretation this means that, for example, officials may NOT consult a video camera that is located at the top of the bleachers."

With that in mind Stigliano spells out in his memo the steps to be taken by officials in case of a last-second-shot controversy. The officials Saturday at Hardin-Simmons followed that procedure exactly. They determined which official would have the responsibility for the last-second call, and the responsible official then made the call.

Harp said a tape of the game has been sent to Stigliano. He will see on the tape that his officials handled the situation correctly. But it will be left to the interpretation whether or not they made the correct call.

Saturday's game at Hardin-Simmons, however, could have been the first test of the new rule allowing instant replay to determine a last-second game-determining basket. Whether right or wrong, it wasn't.

Today, checking the monitor at courtside is commonplace. But some 25-plus years ago, obviously that wasn't the case.

Hold the Press

If a news outlet announces a breaking story these days, it is probably done on X (formerly known as Twitter) or Facebook, Instagram or some other form of social media because it can break its news immediately.

That was not the case thirty years ago.

This is the story of a breaking story that I had to wait twenty-four hours to make the announcement and actually talked another newspaper to hold the story for twenty-four hours, too.

First the background:

One of the biggest sports stories in Abilene, Texas, in the early 1990s was Andrae Patterson, the most heavily recruited basketball player in the city's history. I first heard about Andrae when stories started to come out about this eighth-grader at Madison Middle School who was dunking in games.

I then had a chance to follow Andrae at Abilene Cooper High School, where he was a four-year starter and became the school's all-time leading scorer. In fact, our son, who was a couple of years older than Andrae, played on a summer-league team with him the summer after Andrae's freshman year.

I remember telling Troy, "Someday you can say you played with a future NBA player."

Andrae, a six-foot-nine forward, became a *Parade* all-American at Cooper, played four years at Indiana University, was a second-round pick in the NBA draft by the Minnesota Timberwolves, and played two years in the NBA and nine years of professional basketball in Europe. He is now the assistant general manager of the Portland Trailblazers.

As a sophomore at Cooper, Andrae began drawing the attention of the nation's top college basketball programs. Coaches from Duke, North Carolina, Indiana and Michigan, just to name a few, found their way to Abilene to try to woo Andrae to their schools.

The summer after Andrae's sophomore year, Indiana assistant Dan Dakich scheduled a trip to Abilene. Dennis Harp, Hardin-Simmons University men's basketball coach at the time, is an Indiana native and was friends with members of the Hoosiers' staff. Dakich called Harp to pick him at the Abilene Regional Airport, but Harp and his family were on vacation, so he asked if I would pick up Dakich at the airport.

That developed a friendship that paid dividends over the next year. I got to write a feature then about the time that Dakich, who had been a player at Indiana, held Michael Jordan to fourteen points as the Hoosiers upset North Carolina in the NCAA Tournament.

Dakich said he didn't learn he would be guarding Jordan until the team's shoot-around the morning of the game.

"What did you do when you found out you would be guarding one of the greatest players to ever play the game?" I asked.

"I went back to the hotel and threw up," Dakich quipped.

Indiana head coach Bob Knight came to Abilene that fall to watch Cooper in a preseason practice. Thanks to my relationship with Dakich, I was able to get an exclusive interview with Knight for a story that was front-page news in the *Abilene Reporter-News.*

Later that season, Dakich came back to Abilene to watch Andrae in a game against cross-town rival Abilene High. He and I sat together at the game as more than 4,000 fans jammed into Abilene Christian University's Moody Coliseum to see the Cougars and Eagles battle it out.

It was a Tuesday night in the summer following Andrae's junior year at Cooper when my phone rang at home. It was nearly 11 p.m., and I was already in bed. Tuesdays were an early press time for the newspaper because of the grocery stores insert package, so I wasn't working that night.

It was Dakich calling me to tell me that Andrae, who had been attending Indiana's basketball camp, had committed to the Hoosiers.

"Andrae and his parents are driving back to the hotel," he told me. "You can reach them in about an hour."

Dakich gave me the phone number to the hotel they were staying in.

"But we are already past our deadline," I said.

'You can do whatever you want," he replied, "but I have only given the story to you and the Bloomington paper."

Dakich gave me the phone number of the assistant sports editor of the Bloomington paper. I called, explained my situation and asked if there was any way he could hold the story for a day. Surprisingly, he agreed, although it may have been past his deadline, too.

So at midnight, I called the hotel and got an interview with Andrae, ending the long speculation of where he would be going to school.

All the next day, I worried if my "scoop" would hold. Would the TV stations in Abilene or the news media in Indianapolis break the story before it would appear in our Thursday morning paper?

Thankfully, it held and the Bloomington paper and I had our breaking story – more than twenty-four hours after we were first given the "scoop."

Breaking stories were one of the most enjoyable things about being a sports reporter. It is the competitive challenge that made it fun. I will always be appreciative to Dakich, who has gone on to a broadcasting career in Indianapolis and the Big Ten network, for giving me that unique "scoop."

It was a lesson in developing friendships and trusted sources.

No Play,
No Meal Money

The late Norris Fox of Bald Knob, Arkansas, was a big-time college basketball referee who also happened to be a good friend.

Fox worked in the Southwest Conference for a couple of years. He officiated in other college conferences, too, including the Arkansas Intercollegiate Conference. He also worked the NAIA national tournament in Kansas City numerous times.

In addition to officiating basketball, Fox worked for a company that organized trips for international teams that came to the United States to play preseason games against American college teams, a practice that used to be very common. He traveled with the international teams, handling their travel itinerary, in addition to officiating their games.

He provided me with a number of interesting stories over the years. For example, he was in Bloomington, Indiana, with the Senegal team that was scheduled to play Bob Knight's Hoosiers that night, when the Senegal coach came to him in the hotel.

"Fox, we have a problem," Norris recalled, wondering what the problem could be.

It was typical gray, overcast day in Indiana.

"It is four o'clock, and we are supposed to pray to the east," the coach said. "Which direction is east?"

But my favorite story with Fox came a day after a game I had watched on television.

The Soviet Union Junior National Team was playing a series of exhibition games across the United States against top high school players. They were facing the Arkansas Wings, an AAU team comprised of the best high school players in Arkansas. The game was played at the University of Central Arkansas in Conway, and a Little Rock television station televised it live. I was watching at home.

With about ten or eleven seconds remaining in the game and the Arkansas Wings leading by one point, a Soviet player hit a driving layup down the lane. Fox's partner, Jesse Gatewood, called charging on the play and wiped out the basket that would have given the Soviet team the one-point lead.

The Soviet coach – and his interpreter – came out on the court to argue. It appeared that the Soviet coach was going to pull his team off the court. But, after a lengthy discussion, the Soviet team stayed on the court and allowed the Wings to score an uncontested final basket.

The next day I called Fox.

"What did you tell the Soviet coach?" I asked Fox.

"Eastern European teams will often walk off the court before the end of the game if they don't like a call," he replied. "I told the interpreter to tell him (the Soviet coach) that *"no play, no meal money."*

I sent that story to the Associated Press, and Fox said he received newspaper clippings with that story from friends in Atlanta, Baltimore and other cities around the country.

Several months later, Fox called to tell me the "rest of the story." He had been to an island off the coast of Spain to officiate the 19-and-under World Championships. Fox said he arrived a day early and was attending a reception when the Soviet coach came up to him and gave him a big hug like a long-lost friend.

And the coach spoke perfect English. No need for an interpreter this time. But "no play, no meal money" was certainly an interesting anecdote to the Cold War.

A Determined Hop

Inspirational stories can come from anywhere. This is a story that was told to me that I turned into a one of my favorite columns as reprinted from the June 5, 1998, issue of the *Abilene Reporter-News:*

Fans at the Wylie Little League field at Kirby Lake Park received the shock – and thrill –of their lives recently.

Just when you think you have seen it all in nearly a lifetime of playing, coaching, watching and covering baseball from the Little League to the professional level, along comes one of those stories which tugs at your heartstrings and makes you appreciate the indomitable spirit of those who refuse to let a handicap stop their pursuit of athletic competition.

Taylor County district attorney James Eidson, whose son plays in the Wylie Little League, brought my attention to just such as story this week.

It happened during a minor league baseball game May 27 between the Warriors and the Bombers.

"One of the Warriors is twelve-year-old Bryson Hurt,"

Eidson said. "Bryson is a typical Little Leaguer except for just a couple of things. Due to birth defects, he has only three fingers on his right hand, and only half of his right leg. But Bryson doesn't let that slow him down. Bryson motors down the base paths as well as most and better than some."

Eidson said that the players and parents tend to forget that Bryson is handicapped, which, of course, is just the way Bryson wants it.

An unusual thing happened in the Warriors' game on May 27, however.

Bryson singled into right field in the fourth inning and then stole second base. On the next pitch, Bryson tried to take third base when the catcher bobbled the ball. But the catcher quickly recovered and threw to third, which resulted in Bryson getting caught in a rundown.

During the rundown, Bryson's prosthesis came off, and he fell to the ground. But he didn't stay down.

"At first he crawled, then he jumped up on his good leg and began hopping toward third," Eidson said. "The second baseman wasn't close enough to make the tag, so he threw to third, just as Bryson dove head-first for the bag. He barely beat the throw and was safe at third."

As Bryson lay motionless on third base in exhaustion, Eidson said the Bomber fans gasped in shock. The Bomber shortstop stared down at the prosthesis clad with a baseball shoe and stirrup sock lying between second and third, and he began "backing" into left field.

As coaches from both dugouts ran on to the field to lend a hand, the Warriors' fans began to cheer loudly.

No longer embarrassed, Bryson got up, reattached his leg and smiled at his mother. No doubt she – and a lot of others – were fighting back tears.

The story doesn't end there, either. The next batter got a hit, Bryson scored from third base and the Warriors eventually won the game by one run.

The outcome of the game will probably soon be forgotten. But the lesson that Little League baseball tries to teach about doing your best no matter what the circumstances should stay with everyone in attendance that night at Kirby Lake Park for years to come.

You've taught us all a valuable lesson, Bryson, Congratulations.

Postgame

When the game is over, the real work begins for the sports writer. There is catching coaches or key players for quick quotes, compiling the statistics and writing the story, sometimes in a hurried fashion in which you only have thirty minutes to make the newspaper's deadline.

It is an adrenaline rush, trying to best describe the game and put what happened into context in a short amount of time. You are writing for not only those who weren't at the game who want to know what happened but also for those who were at the game but want to know more or want to know what you had to say about their team. Speed and accuracy are the hallmark of sports writers working on deadline.

The deadline for a sportscaster is much easier, but I always tried to recap the scoring plays and provide final statistics in my postgame wrap-up, giving a proper recap for those who may not have listened to the entire game.

I guess this book could be considered my postgame. I didn't keep many clippings of stories – I have written thousands of stories – through my fifty-year career, but this book was designed to recall some of most favorite memories and unusual games.

Although I am still broadcasting Hardin-Simmons University football and basketball games and still occasionally covering a game or writing a feature, as well as serving as chairman of the Big Country Athletic Hall of Fame, I am slowly winding down my career. Retirement isn't yet part of my vocabulary, so maybe that is why I wanted to recap what has been my life in sports.

I hope you find it entertaining. And for readers of a certain age, they will remember when reading the sports section in the morning newspaper was every bit as important as having that bowl of cereal at the breakfast table. I am sad to see the demise of the newspaper industry.

Whether it was Little League or high school, college or professional sports, there was a joy in covering the variety of sports and trying to bring excitement to the reporting of each of those events. If I was there, It Must Have Been A Big Game.

APPENDIX

Big Country Athletic Hall of Fame

In 1988, I served on the selection committee for an Abilene Independent School District hall of fame. It lasted only two years, however, as a new superintendent had no interest in continuing it.

I thought it was a great thing, however, and in 2002, just after I had left the *Abilene Reporter-News*, Nancy Paup with Texas State Technical College called about a golf tournament to raise money for the TSTC scholarship program. I told her we needed a hall of fame, and the Big Country Athletic Hall of Fame was born to honor the great athletes and coaches from the nineteen-county Big Country area. I have served as chairman since 2002.

It helped raise money for TSTC until 2010 when the Hall of Fame became a non-profit 501c3 organization with its own board of directors. In 2012, the Hall of Fame began awarding college scholarships and has now given out $180,000 in scholarships to graduating seniors.

In 2020, in the middle of the COVID pandemic we moved our museum from the AISD administration building to the Mall of Abilene, where it is open seven days a week free of charge. The museum also holds a reception at the end of each sports season to honor the state medalists from the Big Country.

As of 2025, a total of 251 people have been inducted into the Big Country Athletic Hall of Fame. Videos and photos of the Hall of Fame inductees are available at www.bigcountryhalloffame. org. Here are brief capsules of the remarkable athletes and coaches who have called the Big Country home:

Johnny Agan, Albany – played running back at Albany and Texas Tech and played on two state championship teams at Albany.

Cory Aldridge, Abilene – played football and baseball at Cooper and enjoyed a seventeen-year professional baseball career, including stints in MLB with the Braves, Royals and Angels.

Gene Alford, Rising Star – played in Texas Tech's first football game in 1925 and also played in the NFL.

Randy Allen, Abilene – played football and baseball at Cooper. He coached football at Ballinger, Brownwood, Cooper and Highland Park. He has won four state championships at Highland Park and is now the second winningest coach in Texas high school football history.

Bill Anderson, Stamford – played football at Stamford and coached football at a number of Big Country high schools. The football stadium at Stamford is named for him.

Kendra Anderson-Whitehead, Colorado City – was the NCAA Division III basketball player of the year at Hardin-Simmons where she was an all-American and is now the head coach at her alma mater, leading the Cowgirls to the Sweet 16 in 2024.

Twyman Ash, Abilene – played football at Abilene High and Rice. He caught the winning touchdown pass for the Eagles in the 1954 state championship game.

Michi Atkins, Loraine – was a member of the Texas Tech

Lady Raiders' national championship team in 1993 and is the all-time leading scorer in Southwest Conference basketball history.

Jerale Badon, Abilene – is leading receiver in Abilene High and Abilene Christian University football history.

JimAnne Baker-Hejny, Cisco – played basketball and ran track at Cisco and TCU. She won five gold medals at the state track meet as a senior in 2003 to finish her high school career with 13 gold medals at the UIL state track meet.

Beverly Ball, Abilene –was the swim coach for Abilene High, Cooper and McMurry for more the fifty years.

Kim Bartee-Fuentes, Albany – ran track at Albany and Abilene Christian University, where she was an NCAA Division II national champion in the high jump.

Sammy Baugh, Sweetwater – was quarterback for TCU and the Washington Redskins. He coached at Hardin-Simmons and the New York Jets. He was an inaugural member of the Pro Football Hall of Fame. In 1943, he led the NFL in passing, punting and interceptions as a two-way player.

Emory Bellard, Breckenridge – won two state championships as the coach at Breckenridge and one at San Angelo Central. He invented the wishbone offense while an assistant coach at the University of Texas. Later served as head coach at Texas A&M and Mississippi State.

Dean Berry, Abilene – played football at Cooper and Texas A&M. He was a member of the first 12th Man kickoff team at Texas A&M.

Greg Berry, Abilene – played football at Cooper and Texas A&M.

Powell Berry, Snyder – father of the three Berry brothers. He played quarterback at Snyder and Texas A&M.

Ray Berry, Abilene – played linebacker at Cooper, Baylor and seven years in the NFL, mostly in Minnesota. He led the Vikings in tackles one year and is a member of the Baylor Hall of Fame.

Frank Biggers, Colorado City – all-state basketball player at Wallace High School in Colorado City before integration where his team won 103 games in a row. He averaged 32 points a game as the third leading scorer in the nation at Cisco Junior College. He also played basketball for the Harlem Stars.

Blackie Blackburn, Abilene – a native of Breckenridge who was a long-time baseball coach at Abilene High. He won two state championships with the Eagles.

James Blackwood, Abilene – ran track at Abilene High and Abilene Christian University. He coached track and football at the University of Texas and was head track coach at Texas-San Antonio. He was a longtime associate director of the Texas Relays and five NCAA championships.

Mary Bolden-Washington, Hamlin – was a three-time state champion in the long jump and 4x200 relay at Hamlin and also won gold medals in the 200, triple jump and 4x100 relay. She helped the University of Texas win NCAA national indoor championships in 1986 and 1988. A three-time all-American, she placed fourth in the 200 at the 1984 U.S. Olympic trials and was MVP of the 1987 Texas Relays.

David Bourland, Abilene – played football and baseball at Abilene High and Texas Tech. He was the quarterback of the Eagles' state championship football team in 1955 and played on Abilene High's state championship baseball team in 1956.

Don Bridges, Abilene – was a high school and college basketball referee from 1955-84 and a high school and college football official from 1962-94.

Art Briles, Rule – quarterbacked Rule to the Class B state final and led Rule to the state track championship as a senior. He won four state championships as the head football coach at Stephenville and then served as head football coach at the University of Houston and Baylor.

Ahmad Brooks, Abilene – played football at Abilene High and the University of Texas, where he was a four-year starter as a defensive back. He also played in the NFL.

Jody Brown, Cross Plains – played football and ran track at Cross Plains. He played in four bowl games for Texas Tech and played in the first-ever Big 12 football game.

Doyle Brunson, Sweetwater – was a state champion in the mile. He played basketball at Sweetwater and Hardin-Simmons University. He became the world's most famous poker player. Known as "Texas Dolly", he was a ten-time champion of the World Series of Poker.

Bonnie Buchanan-Gray, May – star basketball player at

May and an all-American at Abilene Christian University. She has 10 of the top individual scoring games in the UIL history of six-on-six girls basketball. In 1976 and 1977, she scored 74, 69, 67, 63, 59 three times, 58 twice and 56 points in individual games.

Wally Bullington, Abilene – longtime football coach and athletic director at Abilene High and Abilene Christian University.

Ron Butler, Ranger – longtime men's and women's basketball coach, softball coach and athletic director at Ranger College.

John Paul Cain, Sweetwater – golfer at Sweetwater and Texas Tech. He was a two-time winner on the Senior PGA Tour.

Jimmy Carmichael, Brownwood – former quarterback at Brownwood and Texas Tech. He threw for 2,308 yards and 28 touchdowns in 1969 to lead Brownwood to the Class 3A state championship. He was a three-year letterman at Texas Tech.

Bob Carothers, Abilene – all-state baseball player at Abilene High who played baseball in the Los Angeles Dodgers' organization.

Jimmy Carpenter, Abilene – former football and baseball player at Abilene High and the University of Oklahoma. He scored both touchdowns in the Eagles' 1956 state championship game.

Judy Casey, Abilene – graduated from Abilene High and was one of the most decorated amateur golfers in Big Country history. She was a three-time winner of the Texas Publinx championship and the West Texas Women's Championship.

Elijah Childers, Abilene – played football, basketball and ran track at Woodson High School in Abilene and played football at Prairie View A&M. He later played in the NFL.

Kenneth Cleveland, Coleman – played basketball at Coleman and the University of Texas. He coached basketball at Dimmitt, where he won twenty-seven districts titles, made eleven state tournament appearances and won three state championships.

Mike Cochran, Stamford – longtime reporter for the Associated Press. He was the author of several books, including Doyle Brunson's biography and the Walker Railey murder trial. Also served as a pallbearer at Lee Harvey Oswald's funeral while covering the events following John F. Kennedy's assassination.

Tonto Coleman, Roscoe – played and coached football at Abilene Christian University and later served as the commissioner of the Southeastern Conference.

Dick Compton, Colorado City – played football at Colorado City, McMurry and in the NFL, including the Pittsburgh Steelers and Detroit Lions.

Charles Coody, Stamford – played golf at Stamford and TCU. He enjoyed a lengthy, successful career on the PGA and PGA Champions tours. He won the coveted green jacket as the winner of the 1971 Masters.

Hall of Famers Charles Coody and Max Williams with Al.

Callie Corley-Ashley, Abilene – a three-sport standout at Abilene High in volleyball, basketball and track, twice qualifying for the state track meet in the 100 hurdles. She played volleyball at TCU where she still ranks second in career digs.

Paula Corn, Baird – scored a record 61 points in the 1964 Class 1A girls state basketball championship game as she led Baird to the state title.

Lynn Corn, Abilene Wylie – led Wylie to the Class 3A girls state basketball championship and was named Ms. Texas Basketball as the state's top player in 1990. She then played for Stephen F. Austin and hit a game-winning shot for the Lady Jacks in an NCAA tournament game.

Harry Craft, Throckmorton – played centerfield for the Cincinnati Reds in 1937-42. He was Mickey Mantle's first minor league manager in Joplin, Mo. He was the manager of the Kansas City A's in 1958-59 and was the Houston Astros' (Colt 45s) first manager from 1962-64.

Barbara Crousen, Abilene – was track coach at Cooper and McMurry University. She is the only female coach to win an NCAA championship coaching a men's team, leading the McMurry men to the NCAA Division III national outdoor track and field championship in 2008 and 2012.

Joe Crousen, Breckenridge – played on a state championship football team at Breckenridge. He had a long high school and college coaching career including head coaching stints at Athens, Ranger College and McMurry University.

Sonny Cumbie, Snyder – led the nation in passing as a senior at Texas Tech in 2004 and was the MVP of the Holiday Bowl when the Red Raiders upset Aaron Rogers and California. He is now the head football coach at Louisiana Tech.

Eck Curtis, Anson – played football at Abilene Christian University. He was the head football coach at Anson, Electra, Ranger and Breckenridge and spent 20 years as an assistant coach at the University of Texas.

Charlie Davis, Stamford – all-state selection at Stamford in 1952 and 1953 and a two-time Little All-American at McMurry. He later coached at Graham, Anson, Rotan and Olney

Don Davis, Stamford – played on two state championship football teams at Stamford and went to the state track meet. Named a Little All-American at McMurry and later coached at Cleburne and Lorenzo.

Ernie Davis, Stamford – all-state football player at Stamford. He was a Little All-American at McMurry where is the 13th leading rusher in school history. He coached at Slaton. All three Davis brothers are in the McMurry Hall of Honor.

Tony Degrate, Snyder – all-American defensive end at the University of Texas. He won the Lombardi Award as nation's top lineman in 1984. He was drafted by the Cincinnati Bengals and played for the Green Bay Packers in the NFL.

Larry Dippel, Stamford – played football at Stamford and Hardin-Simmons University. He posted a 253-73-6 record in 35 seasons as the head football coach at Hereford and Amarillo High.

Spike Dykes, Ballinger – longtime high school and college football coach, including the head coach at Texas Tech from 1986-1999.

Mickey Early, Rotan – played football and ran track at Rotan and played defensive back at SMU. He played briefly for the Houston Oilers before beginning a lengthy career as a principal and superintendent at Rotan and Roby.

Darcell Edwards, Coleman – won six NCAA Division III national championships in the long jump and triple jump from 2001-2004 at McMurry University.

Lawrence Elkins, Brownwood – all-around athlete at Brownwood and a two-time all-American receiver at Baylor. He was selected as the second overall pick in the first round of the AFL draft by the Houston Oilers in 1965.

Margaret Ellison, Abilene – founded and coached the Texas Track Club, an all-girls track team in Abilene known as the "Bouffant Belles" that appeared on the cover of *Sports Illustrated* in 1963.

Dr. Bob Estes, Abilene – star running back on Abilene High's first state championship football team in 1923. He played baseball at Hardin-Simmons University and was a long-time doctor in Abilene.

Bob Estes, Abilene – basketball player and state champion golfer at Abilene Cooper. He won the Nicklaus Award as the nation's top collegiate golfer at the University of Texas and was a four-time winner on the PGA Tour.

Jay Estes, Abilene – basketball and baseball player at Abilene Cooper. He was a starting outfielder on Cooper's 1987 state championship baseball team. He played baseball at Hardin-Simmons University and Texas A&M.

Bobbie Estes, Abilene – wife of Tommy and mother of Bob and Jay. She is the matriarch of the Legacy Award-winning Estes family.

Tommy Estes, Abilene – played football at Abilene High. He coached basketball and golf at Abilene Cooper and McMurry University, including leading the Cooper golf team to three consecutive state championships.

John Ford, Breckenridge – was second in the nation with 1,777 passing yards in 1950 as the quarterback at Hardin-Simmons University. He threw 48 touchdown passes in his collegiate career at HSU.

Ken Ford, Breckenridge – led the nation in passing at Hardin-Simmons University in 1957. He threw for 3,546 yards and 29 touchdowns at HSU and played for the New York

Giants and New York Jets.

Trey Forkerway, Abilene – a three-sport standout in football, basketball and baseball at Abilene High. He played baseball at Texas Tech and minor league baseball in the Chicago Cubs organization and then became a pro baseball scout for the Cubs.

Hollis Gainey, Colorado City – ran on relay teams at the University of Texas that set three world records. He was a long-time coach and assistant athletic director in Lubbock.

Gerald Galbraith, Abilene – played football on Abilene High's Team of the Century football team that won three state championships and 49 games in a row in the 1950s.

Cecil, Gene, Gervis Sr. and R.B. Galbraith, Abilene – brothers who played on Abilene High's state championship football teams in the 1920s and 1930s, beginning a tradition that includes three generations of Galbraiths who excelled in sports in the Abilene ISD.

Gervis Galbraith, Jr., Abilene – a quarterback and defensive back on Abilene High's Team of the Century in the 1950s.

Debs Garms, Bangs – played 12 seasons for the Browns, Braves and Cardinals. He broke Johnny Vander Meer's hitless streak in 1938 and won the National League batting title in 1940.

Joe Gerald, Sweetwater – played football at Sweetwater and Baylor. He was valedictorian of his high school class and became an orthopedic surgeon.

Pat Gerald, Sweetwater – long-time football coach at

Sweetwater from 1945-57 and the father of three generations of the Gerald family as the first Legacy Award recipients.

Pat Gerald, Sweetwater – all-state football player guard/linebacker at Sweetwater on the first Mustangs' team to play in the state championship game in 1957. He played football at Rice University and was long-time bank president in Sweetwater.

Patrick Gerald, Sweetwater – Class 4A all-state linebacker at Sweetwater. He played football at Rice University and Texas Tech.

Kim Gidley, Abilene – played and coached tennis at Abilene High. She was an all-American tennis player at Abilene Christian University and Southern Illinois-Edwardsville. She spent 25 years as the tennis coach at the Air Force Academy.

Bill Gilbreth, Abilene – played baseball at Abilene Christian Schools and Abilene Christian University. He was ACU's first coach when the school brought back baseball. He was a pitcher for three years for the Detroit Tigers and California Angels.

Kathryn Scott Gilreath, Abilene – played No. 1 singles at Abilene Cooper leading the Cougars to three consecutive team tennis state championships. She was a four-year letterman at Texas A&M and won a Big 12 title at No. 5 singles. She coached Wylie to 10 team tennis state championships.

Jerry Don Gleaton, Brownwood – all-American left-handed pitcher with a 13-1 record at the University of Texas in 1979. He was relief pitcher from 1979-92 for the Rangers, Mariners, White Sox, Royals, Tigers and Pirates.

John Ray Godfrey, Aspermont – all-American basketball player and Southland Conference player of the year at Abilene Christian University where he scored 1,467 points. He was the first player to have his jersey number retired at ACU. He was invited to the 1968 U.S. Olympic tryouts.

Julie Goodenough, Haskell – played basketball at Western Texas College and Texas-Arlington. As of 2025, she had won 539 games as the head women's basketball coach at Hardin-Simmons University, Oklahoma State, Charleston Southern and Abilene Christian University.

Elmer Gray, Roscoe – was the first Abilene Christian University athlete to qualify for the U.S. Olympic Trials in the half-mile in 1932. The track stadium at ACU is named for him.

Myrle Greathouse, Abilene – was an all-state football player at Amarillo and an all-American at the University of Oklahoma. A long-time oilman and philanthropist in Abilene, the Big Country Fellowship of Christian Athletes all-star football game is named in his honor.

Merrill Green, Abilene – played on two national championship football teams at the University of Oklahoma. He coached at Abilene Cooper from 1965-71, leading the Cougars to the 1976 state championship game. He then coached for 20 years at Bryan, where the stadium now carries his name. His career coaching record is 197-81-9.

Fred Green, Abilene – played football and baseball on the Team of the Century state championship teams at Abilene

High. He still holds the record for the most RBIs in the high school state tournament.

Oris Greever, Abilene – longtime high school football official who was the referee in the first Crosstown Showdown between Abilene High and Cooper.

Glynn Gregory, Abilene – all-state running back in football and catcher in baseball on the Team of the Century state championship teams at Abilene High. He also played football at SMU and for the Dallas Cowboys.

Bill Grissom, Winters – star running back and defensive back at McMurry University. He was a high school football and track coach for more than 30 years at Hamlin, Colorado City, Breckenridge and Stanton. He won two state track championships at Hamlin.

Ike Groce, Abilene – considered the Father of Tennis in Abilene. He was the middle school tennis coordinator for the Abilene ISD and later coached tennis in Brownwood and Oklahoma State, where he won six Big Eight championships.

Bob Groseclose, Abilene High – won three state track championships as the track coach at Abilene High and was an assistant coach on the Eagles' Team of the Century football team. He then spent 29 years as the track and field coach at Northeast Louisiana, winning numerous conference titles.

Lari Dee Guy, Clyde – won 11 consecutive AJRA roping titles beginning at age 9. She is an eight-time Women's Professional Rodeo World Champion in breakaway roping. She still trains horses, gives roping clinics and is a member of the Texas Cowboy Hall of Fame and the National Cowgirls Hall of Fame.

Sam Harrell, Brownwood – played quarterback at Brownwood. He won 239 games as a high school football coach, including a 203-79 record and three state championships in 23 years as the coach at Ennis.

Jon Harrison, Abilene – wide receiver at Abilene Cooper and the University of Oklahoma. He caught two TD passes for the Sooners in the 1971 Game of the Century against Nebraska. Still holds the OU record for most yards per reception. He was a long-time assistant coach at Bryan, Ballinger and Cooper.

Bob Harrison, Stamford – all-state football player on a state championship team at Stamford and an all-American linebacker on a national championship team at the University of Oklahoma. He was a finalist for the Heisman Trophy in 1958 and played for the 49ers, Eagles and Steelers in the NFL.

Chuck Harrison, Abilene – played football and baseball at both Abilene High and Texas Tech. He played defensive end in Texas Tech's first-ever game in the Southwest Conference. He played first base for the Houston Astros and Kansas City, where he was the starting first baseman in the Royals' first-ever game in 1969.

Leslie Harrison, Stamford – part of the only all-girl rodeo team at Hardin-Simmons to make the National Intercollegiate Rodeo Association finals. She won the American Quarter Horse

Association's World Championship Bayer Select Amateur barrel race six times and the reserve world champion twice. She also won six National Barrel Horse Association senior 1-D champion titles and won seven championships in the open category.

Bill Hart, Baird – longtime sports writer of the *Abilene Reporter-News* who was considered the leading authority on Big Country high school sports. The Legends Award in the Hall of Fame is named in his honor.

Brandon Hawk, Clyde –was twice named the top junior tennis player in Texas, winning five doubles and one singles national titles. He was a freshman all-American and the Big 12 Freshman of the Year at the University of Texas. He then turned professional, winning three singles titles, 11 doubles titles and played in the main draw at the U.S. Open three times and Wimbledon once.

Curly Hays, Abilene – longtime high school and college football and basketball official. The Texas Association of Sports Officials annual award for the state's top referee is named for Hays.

Nikki Heath, Sweetwater – all-state volleyball and basketball player at Sweetwater. She was a starting guard on the Texas Tech Lady Raiders' national championship basketball team in 1993.

Jay Hess, Eastland – Texas High School Player of the Year who threw for 3,154 yards and 37 touchdowns in leading Eastland to the 1982 state title. He ended his high school career with a state-record 5,771 passing yards and 63 TDs. He later played at Texas A&M and the University of Iowa.

Joel Hood, Abilene – assistant coach at Abilene Christian University in 1984 and 1985 when the Wildcats won back-to-back national championships. For the next 20 years, he has been a high school track coach at White Deer, Fort Worth Western Hills, Bowie, Rotan, Rising Star, Roby and Jacksboro.

Derek Hood, Abilene – coached track at Keller Fossil Ridge and Keller Central as well as Bethany College in Kansas. He led ACU men's cross country team to back-to-back NCAA Division II national championships in 2006 and 2007.

Don D. Hood, Abilene – won four NCAA Division II outdoor national track and field championships as the head coach at Abilene Christian University and has also coached at Brownwood, Texas State, LeTourneau University and Harding University.

Don Hood, Abilene – track coach who led the Abilene Christian University to eight NCAA Division II national championships and two NAIA titles. He was considered the nation's top pole vault coach. He mentored 16 Olympians in his career and coached 13 pole vaulters over the 18-foot barrier.

Harold Hudgens, Ballinger – a 6'10" basketball player at Ballinger and Texas Tech. He was drafted in the NBA and ABA but opted to play semi-pro basketball for the Phillips 66ers. He is a member of the Southwest Conference Hall of Fame.

Ray Hudson, Abilene – longtime high school and college football and basketball official. He refereed two Class 5A state championship games and one NCAA Division II national championship game.

Chuck Hughes, Abilene – wide receiver at Abilene High and Texas Western. He set an NCAA record with 401 all-purpose yards in 1965 in the Miners' game against North Texas. He is the only player to die in an NFL game when he suffered a heart attack in 1971 in the Detroit Lions' game against the Chicago Bears.

Dallas Huston, Brownwood – spent 58 years as the recognizable play-by-play voice of Brownwood and Howard Payne football and basketball, winning numerous awards.

Lew Jenkins, Sweetwater – world light heavyweight boxing champion in 1940. He fought in World War II and is buried in Arlington National Cemetery.

Jonathan Johnson, Abilene – broke the state record in the 800 meters and anchored Abilene High's 4x400 relay to a state championship in 2001. He became Texas Tech's first Olympian in 2004 when he won the NCAA championship and the U.S. Olympic Trials in 1:44.77. He reached the semifinals of the 800 at the Olympics in Athens.

Ellis Jones, Abilene – played linebacker at Abilene High, the University of Tulsa and one year in the NFL despite playing with one arm. He was an all-American in 1944 at Tulsa.

Johnny "Ham" Jones, Hamlin – played running back at Hamlin and the University of Texas. He was rushed for 104 yards, including a 32-yard touchdown run, and was named the MVP of the Sun Bowl in 1978.

Rose Mary Jones DeLane, Trent – averaged more than 40 points per game during three seasons at Trent and scored 73 points in a game in 1957. She then played for Wayland Baptist, which won a national AAU championship in 1961 and finished as national runner-up the following two years.

Jimmie Keeling, Abilene – started the football program at Hardin-Simmons in 1990, posting a career record of 172-53 and leading the Cowboys to the national playoffs 11 times. Before HSU, he was a high school coach at Dublin, Tulia, Elgin, Lubbock Estacado, Andrews, Lubbock Coronado, San Angelo Central and Tyler John Tyler. His 1968 Estacado team is the only team in Texas high school history to win a state championship in its first season of varsity football. His career coaching record is 368-144-11.

Louis Kelley, Abilene – running back at Woodson High School in Abilene before integration and at New Mexico State. He was a longtime successful high school football coach at Lubbock Dunbar and Lubbock Estacado.

Kelly Kent, Cisco – all-state running back at Cisco. He played fullback at Abilene Christian where he was named the Outstanding Offensive Player in the NAIA national championship game in 1977 as he rushed for 178 yards and led ACU to the national title.

Hershel Kimbrell, Abilene – played basketball at Abilene High and McMurry University. He was the basketball coach at McMurry from 1959-90, winning 448 games and reaching the postseason 16 times. McMurry's basketball arena is named Hershel Kimbrell Arena.

John Kimbrough, Haskell – star running back on Texas A&M's only national championship football team in 1939. He finished runner-up for the Heisman Trophy that year. He played professional football before and after World War II and served in the Texas legislature.

Rufus King, Abilene – all-state lineman on Abilene High's Team of the Century football team at Abilene High and a three-year letterman and all-Southwest Conference lineman at Rice University.

Mike Kinsey, Brownwood – all-state selection who led Brownwood's stellar defense in the Lions' 14-9 win over Sugar Land Willowridge in the 1981 Class 4A state championship game. He was a four-year starter at Texas Tech at nose guard and linebacker and was named the outstanding player in the 1985 Blue-Gray Senior Bowl.

Lance Kitchens, Breckenridge – has been the Voice of the Buckaroos for 40 years, broadcasting Breckenridge football, basketball, baseball and softball games.

Wes Kittley, Rule – a state champion in the 800 meters in high school and an all-American in the 800 at Abilene Christian University. He is one of the nation's top track coaches, winning 29 NCAA Division II national titles at ACU and two Division I national championships at Texas Tech.

Fred Kniffen, Clyde – state singles champion at Clyde and played tennis at Hardin-Simmons, where he is a member of HSU's hall of honor. He was Cooper's first tennis coach and served as the head tennis pro at Fair Park Tennis Center. He started the tennis tech program at Tyler Junior College in 1973 and won four junior college national championships at Tyler.

John Lackey, Abilene – played football, basketball and baseball at Abilene High. He had a major league career pitching record of 188-147 with 2,294 strikeouts and an earned run average of 3.92. He won World Series rings with the Angels, Red Sox and Cubs, including being the winning pitcher in Game 7 for the Angels in the 2001 World Series, the first rookie since 1909 to accomplish that feat.

Adree Lakey Whitefield, Roby – won state championships in the shot put and discus in high school. She then won NCAA Division II national championships in the shot put, discus and hammer throw at Angelo State.

Bruce Land, Hawley – one of the top sprinters in the nation in the late 1950s. He won a national junior college championship in the 100 at Cisco Junior College and ran at McMurry. He qualified for the 1960 U.S. Olympic Trials in the 100, 200 and long jump.

Lillian Faye Langford, Breckenridge – played semipro basketball in 1929 and 1930 for the Dallas Golden Cyclones. She also competed in track and led her Dallas team to fourth place at the AAU national meet, finishing second in the softball throw, javelin and baseball throw. In 1942, she played baseball for the Rockford Peaches, a team that was featured in the movie "A League of Their Own."

Dr. Lynn Lawhon, Abilene – longtime high school and college football official. He also worked in the NFL during the referees' strike.

Shorty Lawson, Abilene – longtime high school and college football official. He worked the famous Arkansas-Texas game in 1969 that was played in front of President Nixon and led to the Longhorns' national championship. He was also an assistant coach at Abilene High and later athletic director for Abilene ISD.

Lyle Leong, Abilene – a three-sport standout in football, basketball and track at Abilene High, earning all-district honors in all three sports. He had 91 receptions for 1,850 yards and 23 touchdowns and was a two-time state champion in the high jump, clearing 7'1". He also competed in football and track at Texas Tech and had 74 receptions for 926 yards as a senior.

Bob Lilly, Throckmorton – known as Mr. Cowboy and the NFL's top defensive lineman in his era, he was the first draft pick for the Dallas Cowboys, the first Cowboy in the Ring of Honor and the first Cowboy in the Pro Football Hall of Fame.

Steve Lineweaver, Abilene – played baseball at Abilene High but made his mark as a high school football coach. In 22 seasons at Commerce and Euless Trinity, he compiled a 259-43-2 record and won four state championships.

Bill Little, Winters – longtime sports information director at the University of Texas. He was the leading authority on Longhorns sports history, author of several Texas books and also served as the radio voice for Longhorn baseball.

David Little, Abilene – led Abilene High to a 34-5 record and the state basketball tournament in 1978. He scored 1,827 points in four seasons at Texas Tech and the University of Oklahoma and was drafted by the Denver Nuggets.

Mike Little, Abilene – was the youngest of the three Little brothers who played basketball at Abilene High and in the Southwest Conference. He played basketball at Howard College and Baylor.

Richard Little, Abilene – played basketball at Abilene High and Texas Tech. He was two-time first-team all-Southwest Conference selection and played on the Red Raiders 1973 SWC championship team. He is a member of the Texas Tech and SWC Halls of Fame.

Peyton Little Decker, Abilene – scored over 3,000 points in her high school career and led Wylie to the state tournament in 2010 and state championships in 2011 and 2012. In the 2012 title game, she scored 33 points and was named the state tournament MVP. She played basketball at Texas A&M and

Oklahoma and finished her career with 1,187 points during three seasons at OU.

Jerry Don Logan, Graham – was a two-way starter at West Texas State. He led the nation in scoring as a senior and was named the Most Valuable Player of the 1962 Sun Bowl. He was the 47th pick in the 1963 NFL draft by the Baltimore Colts and played in Super Bowls III and V. His late interception sealed the Colts' win over the Dallas Cowboys in Super Bowl V.

Boyce "Boone" Magness, Breckenridge – quarterback for the Breckenridge team that tied Port Arthur 0-0 in a snowstorm in the 1929 state championship game after upsetting Waco in the semifinals. He played quarterback at Washington State and was selected to the inaugural class of the Texas High School Football Hall of Fame.

James Mallon, Abilene – a three-time all-district baseball player at Abilene High where he batted .402. He played two years at Baylor before signing with the San Francisco Giants in 1965. He played five years in the Giants' farm system. He was the head coach at Southwestern University from 1971-2004 where his teams won 1,197 games with only 601 losses. The Pirates finished third in the 1984 NAIA World Series.

Andy Malone, Abilene – posted a 220-52 record in seven seasons at Cooper, winning six district titles and back-to-back state championships in 1987 and 1988. His 1987 team went 33-3 and was named the co-national champions by *Collegiate Baseball*. In 41 years as a high school baseball coach, he compiled an 861-345 record.

Milton Martin, Avoca – was a member of Avoca's 1955 Class B state championship basketball team. He once scored a school-record 62 points in a game. He was the leading scorer in the scholarship era at Hardin-Simmons with 1,584 points in four seasons. He coached basketball for 40 years in Lubbock, Henrietta, Lueders-Avoca and Stamford.

Billy Maxwell, Abilene – won the U.S. Amateur golf tournament in 1951 and was a member of two national championship golf teams at North Texas State. He had a 4-0 record as a member of the U.S. Ryder Cup team in 1964 and claimed seven victories during his PGA Tour career.

Don Maynard, Colorado City – played wide receiver at Texas Western and in the NFL with the New York Giants and Jets. He was a four-time AFL All-Star and played for the Jets' Super Bowl III champions. He is in the Pro Football Hall of Fame with 637 career receptions for 11,824 yards and 88 touchdowns.

Mike McClellan, Stamford – all-state running back on state championship football teams in 1955 and 1956 and a state champion in the 100, 220 and long jump on Stamford's state championship track team in 1957. He was an academic all-American at Oklahoma and the hero of OU's 1961 upset victory over Army when he scored on a 74-yard run. He played two seasons with the Philadelphia Eagles.

Bill McClure, Abilene – spent a 47-year career in athletics, beginning as a coach at Stamford and then as an assistant and later head track coach at Abilene Christian, South Carolina and LSU before finishing his career as the director of athletics at Samford University. He was the assistant track coach for the U.S. Olympic team at the 1972 Olympics in Munich.

Colt McCoy, Tuscola – led Jim Ned to the 2003 Class 2A state championship football game. He threw for 9,344 yards and 116 touchdowns at Jim Ned and is the fourth leading passer in Texas high school history. His record of 45-8 as the Texas Longhorns' starting quarterback is the second most in NCAA history. He was a two-time finalist for the Heisman Trophy.

Jim McKinney, Abilene – Cooper gymnastics coach for 23 years where his teams won three state championships and finished second four times. He coached 38 individual state champions. He was also a noted gymnastics judge, working 120 national championship gymnastics meets, including the U.S. Olympic Trials, the USA Nationals and the NCAA Championships, along with 15 international championship meets.

Robert McLeod, Merkel – one of the top two-sport stars in Big Country history. He is the only player to be selected to the All-Century team at Abilene Christian University in both football and basketball. After college, he played tight end with the Houston Oilers from 1961-66.

Lon McMillin, Haskell – was an outstanding athlete in football and track at Haskell, but he made his mark in boxing. He was the state lightweight Golden Gloves championship in

1938 and had a career boxing record of 64 wins, three losses and two draws.

Rick Meyers, Abilene – a three-time all-state selection at Cooper and the individual state singles champion in 1976, finishing his senior year with a 63-0 record. He played No. 1 singles and doubles on Cooper's two state team tennis championship teams. He was a four-time all-Southwest Conference selection at TCU and played three years on the pro tennis tour, playing in all four Grand Slam events.

Chip Meyers, Abilene – he and partner Ronny Fulwiler won Cooper's first district title of any sport when they captured the district doubles title in 1960. Chip played tennis at Baylor from 1964-68 and was runner-up in the Southwest Conference in doubles in 1968.

Twins Scott and David Meyers, Abilene – were the state doubles champion at Cooper in 1982 and state runner-up in 1983. They played No. 1 doubles on a Cooper team that won a state team title in 1982 and was runner-up in 1981. Scott played tennis at TCU and earned all-Southwest Conference honors at top 10-ranked TCU.

Mike Meyers, Abilene – played tennis for two years at Texas A&M. He was ranked in the top 40 in Texas as a junior tennis player. The five Meyers brothers are considered the First Family of Tennis in Abilene.

Jack Mildren, Abilene – led Cooper to the state championship football game in 1967. He was an all-American wishbone quarterback at Oklahoma and was a Heisman finalist in 1971. He played in the NFL with the Baltimore Colts and New England Patriots and later won election as the lieutenant governor of Oklahoma.

Bill Miller, Winters – won the Class 2A state long jump in 1959 in Winters and captured NAIA championships in the long jump in 1962 and 1963 at McMurry, becoming the first Texan to long jump 26 feet or better. His best jump of 26 feet, 6-3/4 inches earned him a fourth-place finish at the 1964 U.S. Olympic Trials.

Jim Millerman, Abilene – ran on Abilene High's sprint relay team that won a gold medal at the state track meet and recorded the fastest time in the nation in 1954 as the Eagles won the state team championship. Then that fall, Millerman was an all-state running back as AHS won the first of three consecutive state football championships. He later ran track and played football at Baylor.

Colonel Buster Mills, Ranger – lettered in football, basketball, track and baseball at the University of Oklahoma and was named the all-Big Six quarterback. He played 415 games for the Red Sox, Browns, Yankees and Indians and compiled a lifetime batting average of .287 with 14 home runs and 163 runs batted-in.

A.J. "Jack" Mills, Stamford – was quarterback of Stamford's undefeated 1955 Class 2A state championship team. He earned a law degree at Oklahoma and in 1966 went into private law practice in Boulder, Colorado, specializing in the representation of professional athletes, primarily NFL players and pro golfer Hale Irwin. In 1970, he represented four players who were taken in the first round of the NFL draft.

Mike Morris, Abilene – played baseball at Cooper and became a major college umpire in the Big 12 Conference. He has called games in two College World Series and dozens of college regional, super-regional and Big 12 tournaments.

Chuck Moser, Abilene – coached Abilene High to a state record 49-game winning streak and three consecutive state football championships from 1954-56. He had a record of 78-7-2 and six district titles in seven seasons at Abilene High. His overall coaching record was 141-28-2.

Mindy Myers, Munday – won 11 gold medals, two silvers and one bronze medal at the state track meet as the Mogulettes won three state championships. She won two state championships and one second-place finish in guiding Munday to two team titles and a second-place finish in cross country. She also earned all-state tournament honors in leading Munday to one appearance in the Class A state basketball tournament.

Mark Oates, Abilene – won the Class 5A state all-around championship at Abilene High in 1981. He was then a three-time all-American in gymnastics at the University of Oklahoma. He won an NCAA championship in the vault in 1983 and was a member of the USA Gymnastics team in 1988. He just missed making the 1988 U.S. Olympic team.

Billy Olson, Abilene – was the Texas 5A pole vault state champion at Abilene High. He won eight NAIA pole vault championships at Abilene Christian and held 11 world records, including becoming the first vaulter to clear 19 feet. He broke the world indoor record seven times in 1982 and 1983. He was a member of the 1980 U.S. Olympic team that wasn't allowed to compete in Moscow because of the U.S. boycott, and he finished 12th in the pole vault in the 1988 Olympics in Seoul, South Korea.

Terry Orr, Abilene – played running back on Cooper's district championship team and then played for the Texas Longhorns, where he rushed for 1,279 yards and 11 touchdowns. He was selected in the 10th round of the 1985 NFL draft and played tight end for the Washington Redskins and San Diego Chargers. He was a member of the Redskins' Super Bowl-winning teams in both 1987 and 1991.

Ray Overton, Paint Creek – coached football for 15 years at Haskell, the last 10 as the Indians' head coach. He then joined the staff at Abilene Cooper, where he spent 19 years as a coach, the last 11 as the Cougars' head coach, posting a 69-40-2 record. After 19 years in Abilene, he spent 10 more years as the head coach at Irving MacArthur.

David Parks, Abilene – played wide receiver and tight end at Abilene High and Texas Tech. He was the first overall selection in the 1964 NFL draft by the San Francisco 49ers. He led the NFL in receptions, receiving yards and receiving touchdowns in 1965. He is a member of the College Football Hall of Fame.

Brad Parris, Abilene – Abilene High graduate and a three-time NCAA Division III indoor national champion in the pole vault and two-time Division III outdoor national champion at McMurry. He was named the ASC Male Athlete of the Year in 2000 and later was head track coach at his alma mater.

Pug Parris, Abilene – long-time professor at her alma mater McMurry University. She is a veteran volunteer at McMurry track and field meets and continues today as the announcer for home meets. She is the wife of Rickey and mother of Brad as part of the Legacy Award recipients.

Rickey Parris, Abilene – qualified for the state track meet in the pole vault three straight years at Wylie and won the state title in 1968 with a new Class A record of 14'1". He won the Lone Star Conference pole vault three times and NAIA Indoor and outdoor championships in 1971 and 1972. He was the first NAIA pole vaulter to clear 17 feet.

Jack Patterson, Merkel – Southwest Conference champion holder in the high hurdles at Rice. He coached at Merkel and San Angelo, as well as the University of Houston, Baylor and the University of Texas, winning six SWC championships. He spent nine years as athletic director at Baylor where he hired Grant Teaff.

Andrae Patterson, Abilene – a *Parade* basketball all-American at Cooper and leading scorer in school history, a four-year starter at Indiana University and taken in the second round of the NBA Draft by the Minnesota Timberwolves. He played two seasons with the Timberwolves and nine years of professional basketball in Europe. He is now the assistant general manager of the Portland Trail Blazers.

Frank C. Payne Jr., Breckenridge – a three-year letterman in football from 1943-45, serving as the Buckaroos' starting quarterback as a junior and halfback as a senior, before breaking his leg in the final minutes of the season opener. Breckenridge won the district championship all three years.

Jim Payne, Breckenridge – played on district championship teams at Breckenridge in 1946 and 1947 when the Buckaroos lost in the state semifinals. He also played quarterback at Tarleton State, Cisco Junior College and SMU. He coached in Odessa and Corsicana before going into school administration.

Ron Payne, Breckenridge – all-state lineman from 1955-57 at Breckenridge. He caught a pass to score the first two-point conversion in Texas history. He played defensive end, linebacker and offensive end from 1959-61 at the University of Oklahoma and played and coached for nine years for the Calgary Stampeders in the Canadian Football League.

Jerry Payne, Breckenridge – all-state end on Breckenridge 1954 state championship team. He was a three-year letterman on three consecutive Big Eight championship teams from 1957-59 at Oklahoma. He became a doctor like his father and served in Vietnam.

Dr. Frank Payne Sr., Breckenridge – after serving in World

War II, he was the Breckenridge team doctor from 1946-75. His four sons all played football for the great Buckaroos teams in the 1940s and 1950s.

Stuart Peake, Abilene – was the only player to start every game for all three years on Abilene High's three consecutive state championship teams from 1954-56. Although he played guard, he ran on the Eagles' sprint relay team. He was also a member of Darrell Royal's first recruiting class at the University of Texas.

Al Pickett receiving his HOF Award from fellow Hall of Famer Carlton Stowers in 2016.

Al Pickett, Abilene – spent 15 years as sports editor for the *Abilene Reporter-News* and for the last 25 years has been a high school and Hardin-Simmons play-by-play announcer, a freelance writer, author of six books and the founder and chairman of the Big Country Athletic Hall of Fame.

Taylor Potts, Abilene – is the leading passer in Abilene High history. He threw for 3,162 yards and 53 touchdowns, twice leading the Eagles to the Class 5A regional semifinals. He was a two-year starting quarterback at Texas Tech, throwing for 7,835 yards and 62 touchdowns and was named the offensive MVP of both the 2009 Alamo Bowl and the inaugural Ticket City Bowl in 2011.

Scotty Pugh, Abilene – a four-year starter at first base in baseball for Cooper, he led District 4-5A in home runs as a freshman and earned all-state honors as the Cougars won back-to-back state championships in 1987 and 1988. He was also a three-year starter at quarterback in football and a three-year starter at point guard in basketball. He was a three-year starter at first base at the University of Texas and led the Southwest Conference in batting average as a freshman.

Brad Pursley, Merkel – was a state champion at Merkel and a NAIA and NCAA national champion in the pole vault at Abilene Christian. He competed internationally and qualified for the U.S. Olympic trials three times. He was ranked as high as No. 3 in the world and was ranked among the top five U.S. pole vaulters from 1981-87.

Jackie Ramsey-Cox, Abilene – The 1970 Cooper graduate was one of the top skeet shooters in the country. She won 18 individual and team gold medals at World Championships from 1968-79. She was named an All-American seven times and was the captain of the Ladies all-American team in 1976.

Jon Rhiddlehoover, Abilene – was an all-state lineman and star discus thrower at Cooper and then earned all-Southwest Conference honors as a lineman at the University of Arkansas.

He later coached at Cooper and McMurry.

Dominic Rhodes, Abilene – is the third leading rusher (3,102 yards) in Cooper history and led the Cougars to the state championship game in 1996. He played at Midwestern State and signed as a free agent with the Colts. He was the first undrafted running back to rush for more than 1,000 yards in his rookie NFL season. He rushed for 113 yards and a touchdown in the Colts' Super Bowl XLI victory.

Trey Richey, Jayton – led Jayton to back-to-back undefeated seasons and state championships in 1984 and '85. In the '85 game, he rushed for a state-record 461 yards and eight touchdowns on 28 carries. He played defensive back at McMurry. He is the only person to win a six-man state championship as a player and coach, doing it six times. He won four state championships as the coach at Borden County.

Tom Ritchey, Sweetwater – is the winningest coach in Sweetwater football history. He coached at Sweetwater for 12 years, leading the Mustangs to 11 playoff appearances. His record at Sweetwater was 120-24-2 and his career coaching record is 208-64-7.

Julian "Tex" Robertson, Sweetwater – was member of the 1932 U.S. Olympic water polo team that won a bronze medal. He was the University of Texas' first swim coach from 1935-1950. He trained 13 all-Americans and multiple Olympians and won 13 Southwest Conference championships. He also started Camp Longhorn, a summer camp that still operates today.

Wendell Robinson, Stamford – played on three state championship football teams at Stamford and then played at the University of Oklahoma and Northeastern Oklahoma. He compiled a high school coaching record of 224-110-4 at stops including Santa Anna, Merkel, Spur, Lindale, West Rusk and Bangs.

Brad Rowland, Hamlin – still holds the career rushing record (4,437 yards) at McMurry. He caught the winning touchdown pass for the West in the 1951 East-West Shrine Game. He is in the College Football Hall of Fame and played one year for the Chicago Bears.

David Salas, Abilene – was an all-district cornerback in football and also ran track at Abilene High. His blocked extra point helped the Eagles beat Cooper in overtime in the crosstown showdown in 2001. He is the top soccer player to come out of Abilene and is ranked first all-time at Hardin-Simmons with 46 goals, 115 total points and 17 game-winning goals. He was the American Southwest Conference MVP in 2006.

Dan Salkeld, Abilene – all-state athlete while playing football and basketball and running track at Abilene High. He led the Eagles to the 1928 state championship. After earning his degree from TCU, he had a long coaching career in the Texas high school ranks before retiring in 1975.

Jakie Sandifer, Breckenridge – played on a state championship football team at Breckenridge and a national championship team at the University of Oklahoma. He was a two-year starter at OU and scored the go-ahead touchdown against Texas and scored twice against Duke in the Orange Bowl as a senior. He also ranked third nationally in punt returns in 1958.

Bob Sanderson, Abilene – was the head gymnastics coach at Abilene High from 1983-99, winning a state championship in 1989 and coaching teams that took second once and third twice at the state meet. He was twice named the Texas High School Gymnastics Coach of the Year.

Hugh Sandifer, Abilene – coached at Wylie for 41 years, serving as head basketball coach, head football coach and athletic director. He led the Bulldogs to the state championship game four times, winning the title in 2004. His career football coaching record is 282-109-4. Wylie's football team is named for him.

Ann Schroeder, Abilene – was ranked No. 2 in singles in Texas and No.1 in doubles as a junior tennis player. She was state runner-up in doubles in both 1972 and 1973 and led Cooper to a runner-up finish in the first team tennis state tournament. She played collegiate tennis at Trinity, which won three NCAA Division I national championships, and Schroeder was named an all-American as a senior. She played on the women's professional tennis tour from 1978-81 and achieved a world singles ranking of 148.

Leanne Scott, Abilene – in 17 years as the tennis coach at Cooper from 1987-2004, her teams won 14 district championships. And from 1993-95, the Cougars went 57-0 and won an unprecedented three consecutive Class 5A team tennis state championships. In 2008, she was named to the Texas Tennis Coaches Association Hall of Fame.

Fred Scott, Abilene – won a state doubles title as a senior at Sweetwater. He played tennis at Eastern Kentucky, Amarillo College and Hardin-Simmons. He then coached tennis at Mason, New Braunfels, Sweetwater, North Texas State, Plainview and Abilene High. He was 247-47 as the Abilene High tennis coach, winning 10 district team championships and the 1999 Class 5A state team tennis championship.

Fred L. Scott Sr., Sweetwater – coached football, basketball and tennis for 25 years in Sweetwater and is credited with talking the UIL into having team tennis as a fall sport. Both father and son are in the Texas Tennis Coaches Association Hall of Fame.

James Segrest, Bangs – known as the "One Man Gang from Bangs" when he single-handedly scored 34 points at the 1954 Class A track and field state meet to win the state championship for the Dragons. He ran on relay teams that set five world records from 1956-58 at Abilene Christian. As a track coach, he led Monahans to a state title in 1966, and his teams at Odessa College won 11 National Junior College Athletic Association national championships in indoor and outdoor track.

Cindy Shelton-Raughton, Avoca – played three years for the Wayland Baptist College Hutcherson Flying Queens that won an AAU national championship in 1960. She was also on an all-American team that went to Russia to play in the early 1960s.

Charles Norris Shira, Hamlin – was a star football player at Hamlin. After World War II, he returned to play football at West Point. He spent 10 years as an assistant coach to Darrell Royal at the University of Texas before being named the head football coach and athletic director at Mississippi State.

P.E. "Pete" Shotwell, Abilene – was the first coach to win football state championships at three different schools (Abilene High, Breckenridge and Longview). He began his coaching career at Cisco and, after winning a state championship at Abilene High in 1923, he returned to coach the Eagles from 1946-52.

Dr. William "Dub" Sibley, Abilene – played football at Abilene High and Texas A&M. He was an all-Southwest Conference linebacker and center in 1941 and still holds the conference record for interceptions by a linebacker. As a Marine, he fought in the Battle of Iwo Jima in World War II. He served as the Abilene High football team doctor in the 1950s.

Ted Sitton, Stamford – was the quarterback on Abilene Christian's only unbeaten, untied team that won the Refrigerator Bowl in 1950. He was an assistant coach on ACU's two national championship teams in 1973 and 1977 and was the head coach at ACU from 1978-84. He also coached at Graham and won a state championship as the track coach at Abilene High.

Aultman, Jack and Stanley Smith, Abilene – Aultman, the oldest of the three Smith brothers, led Abilene High to consecutive state championship game appearances. He rushed for 252 yards and three touchdowns in the 1928 state championship game. He went on to play football at Texas A&M. Jack, the middle Smith brother, was also a member of the 1928 state championship football team. He was the leading scorer on the Eagles' basketball team, and, as a senior, won first place in the 120-yard high hurdles, 800-yard run and the high jump at the district track meet. Stanley, the youngest of the three Smith brothers, was an all-state center on the undefeated 1931 state champion Abilene High football team.

Dean Smith, Graham – played football and ran track at the University of Texas. He ran on the gold-medal-winning U.S. 4x100 relay team and took fourth in the 100 at the 1952 Olympics. He became a stuntman and appeared in 10 John Wayne movies. He is in the Hollywood Stuntman Hall of Fame.

Justin Snow, Abilene – was an all-state defensive end at Cooper and defensive end at Baylor before signing with the Indianapolis Colts as a free agent. He was the deep snapper on the Colts' Super Bowl XLI winning team. He and Dominic Rhodes were the first high school teammates to play on a winning Super Bowl team.

Morris, Terry, Si, and Shae Southall, Brownwood – Morris was Hall of Fame coach Gordon Wood's top assistant for 26 years at Brownwood, where the Lions won seven state championships. Two of Brownwood's state championship teams were quarterbacked by Southall's sons Si and Shae. His oldest son Terry was a starting quarterback at Baylor.

Ed Sprinkle, Tuscola – played six-man football at Tuscola and three years at Hardin-Simmons University before World War II. He played 12 years as a guard and defensive end for the Chicago Bears. He is a member of the Pro Football Hall of Fame.

Mike Standly, Abilene – was a state qualifier for three years in high school, playing for Cooper's first state golf title team in 1982. He was an all-American at the University of Houston in 1986 as the Cougars won an NCAA national championship. He played on the PGA Tour from 1991-2008. He had one win, 35 top 25 finishes and 12 top 10 finishes on the PGA Tour.

Tom Stanton, Abilene – was an all-American basketball player at Cooper in 1968, scoring 50 points once in a game. He was a three-year starter in basketball and earned two letters in baseball at Baylor. He was Baylor's athletic director from 1996-2003.

W.T. Stapler, Hamlin – played football at Hamlin and McMurry, but he made his name as a successful high school football coach with more than 200 wins. He led Sweetwater to its only state championship in 1985. He also coached at Conroe, Andrews and Brownwood.

Richard "Moose" Stovall, Abilene – played football at Abilene High and Abilene Christian and was the starting center for the Washington Redskins in 1949 when he snapped the ball to Pro Football Hall of Fame quarterback Sammy Baugh. After his playing career ended, Stovall became a longtime high school and college football referee.

Carlton Stowers, Abilene – was co-captain of the Abilene High track team that won a state championship in 1960 and also ran track at the University of Texas. He became a sports writer for the *Dallas Morning News, Abilene Reporter-News* and *Dallas Cowboys Weekly* and the author of more than 30 books, including a biography of former Cowboys quarterback Roger Staubach.

Jack Stuard, Abilene – was the public address announcer at Shotwell Stadium from 1963-2005. By his count, he missed only four Cooper games at Shotwell Stadium in 43 years, all to travel to watch his son Kyle play for Texas A&M.

Phil Swenson, Avoca – spent 36 years coaching girls basketball and track at Iraan, Wink, Garden City, Hamlin, Winters and Roscoe. He is a member of the Texas Girls Coaches Association Hall of Fame. As a track coach, his teams won two state championships and numerous district and regional titles. He won 447 basketball games.

Jim Taylor, Clyde – was a three-sport star at Clyde. He played center and linebacker, at Baylor. The Pittsburgh Steelers drafted Taylor in the third round of the 1956 NFL draft. He spent one season with the Steelers and two years with the Chicago Cardinals before joining the Hamilton Tiger Cats in the Canadian Football League.

Grant Teaff, Snyder – played football at Snyder and McMurry University and coached football at McMurry, Angelo

State and Baylor. He had a 170-151-8 in 21 seasons as the head coach at Baylor. He was also executive director of the American Football Coaches Association. Tiger Stadium in Snyder was renamed for Teaff.

Al with Hall of Famers Grant Teaff and Ray Berry.

John Thomas, Abilene – was an all-state nose guard and offensive lineman for the 1954 state championship football team at Abilene High. He led the team in tackles. He was a two-time all-American lineman at McMurry.

Trey Todd, Abilene – won back-to-back individual Class 3A state golf championships at Wylie in 2001 and 2002. He was a four-year letterman at Texas A&M, where he had two top 10 finishes and eight top 25 finishes and was named Texas A&M's top scholar athlete for all sports as a senior.

David Tollison, Abilene – was 11-1 as a pitcher and batted .417 with seven home runs and 45 RBIs and 19 stolen bases as a senior on Cooper's state championship baseball team. He was a three-year starter at second base for the Texas Longhorns. He was named first team all-Southwest Conference and second team all-American in 1990, leading the Longhorns with 12 home runs, 21 doubles and 69 RBI while batting .350. He was selected in the sixth round of the MLB draft by the Toronto Blue Jays.

Jerry Tubbs, Breckenridge – played center on two state championship football teams at Breckenridge. He played center and linebacker at the University of Oklahoma. He spent 29 years as a player, player-coach and full-time assistant coach for the Dallas Cowboys.

Jack Turner, Abilene – lost only five times in his boxing career, all in the Golden Gloves state finals. He coached Abilene's Golden Gloves boxing team from 1948-59 and was the first Abilenian to coach the Texas Golden Gloves team at the national tournament. He also served as the Little League baseball district administrator from 1972-1984.

Clyde "Bulldog" Turner, Sweetwater – played football at Sweetwater and Hardin-Simmons. He was an eight-time All-Pro center and linebacker for the Chicago Bears, playing on NFL championship teams in 1940, '41,'43 and '46. He was head coach of the New York Titans in 1962.

C.H. Underwood, O'Brien – was the coach at O'Brien in 1972, the first team to win a UIL six-man state championship. He is the author of two books on six-man football. He also has career record of 356-157 as a high school basketball coach.

Bill Voss, Abilene – was a middle school coach and director of transportation for the Abilene ISD and a longtime football official in the Southwest Conference. He worked as the umpire in numerous bowl games including the Notre Dame-West Virginia game in the Fiesta Bowl.

Steve Warren, Abilene – is the winningest football coach in Abilene High history, compiling 175-68 record in 19 seasons from 1996-2014, including a state championship in 2009. A native of Lockney, Warren had coaching stops at Sweetwater, Wall, Rotan, Rockwall and Grapevine before being hired as an assistant coach at Abilene High in 1994.

Larry Wartes, Stamford – played basketball and baseball at Hardin-Simmons. He was an all-Border Conference guard at HSU in basketball. He won two state football championships as an assistant coach at Stamford and two more as the head coach in 1958 and 1959. He had a 97-47-4 record as head football coach at Stamford and Hereford.

James Washington, Stamford – played wide receiver on two state championship teams at Stamford in 2012 and 2013. He caught 74 passes for 1,549 yards and 13 touchdowns as a senior at Oklahoma State in 2017 in winning the Biletnikoff award as the nation's top receiver. He was selected in the second round of the NFL draft by the Pittsburgh Steelers and caught 114 passes for 1,629 yards and 11 touchdowns during four years with the Steelers.

Jim Welch, Abilene – was a fullback and linebacker on the 1955 state championship team at Abilene High. In his first start at fullback as a senior, he rushed for 233 yards against Odessa

High. He played fullback and linebacker at SMU and then spent nine seasons in the NFL as a defensive back, eight with the Baltimore Colts and one season with the Detroit Lions.

Mike Welch, Sweetwater – was a two-time all-state running back and defensive back at Sweetwater, helping lead the Mustangs to a state championship in 1985. He was a four-year starter at defensive back at Baylor and was named a second-team defensive back on *Dave Campbell's Texas Football Magazine's* 50th anniversary high school football team.

Stanley Whisenhunt, Abilene – longtime girls basketball coach at Wylie. His teams won 15 consecutive district championships and two regional championships, captured third place in the Class A girls basketball state tournament in 1964 and then won the state title in 1970. He was the Wylie superintendent from 1972-85.

Max Williams, Avoca – led Avoca to the 1955 Class B state basketball championship. He was the leading scorer in Texas high school history at the time. He was an all-Southwest Conference guard at SMU and was the first general manager of the Dallas Chaparrals, who became the San Antonio Spurs.

Fred Wolcott, Snyder – was one of the greatest collegiate hurdlers in history at Rice University. He won an NCAA title and broke Jesse Owens' world record in the 220-yard low hurdles. Due to the cancellation of the Olympics during World War II, however, he was denied recognition on the world stage.

Charles Womack, Hawley – coached both boys and girls basketball and served as superintendent at Hawley from 1947-

79. His boys' teams had a record of 896-127 and his girls teams had a 674-110 record. His total of 1,570 wins is a national record for combined victories. His Bearcats won 29 district titles and made 10 state tournament appearances.

Gordon Wood, Brownwood – had 396 wins as a high school football coach, which was the national record at the time of his retirement in 1985. He won two state championships at Stamford and seven at Brownwood, where the football stadium is named in his honor.

Bob Young, Brownwood – played 16 seasons as a lineman in the NFL, mostly with the St. Louis Cardinals. He was named to the Pro Bowl in 1978 and 1979.

Doug Young, Brownwood – was a three-time world powerlifting champion. He was the youngest of the three Young brothers who played football at Brownwood.

Perry Young, Brownwood – played wide receiver and safety on Brownwood state championship teams in 1967 and 1969. He became known as a top fastpitch softball player and spent his career coaching high school girls softball.

John Paul Young, Abilene – offensive lineman at Abilene High and Texas Western. He made his mark as a long-time assistant coach, first at SMU and Texas A&M and then in the NFL with the Oilers, Saints, Chiefs, Broncos and Bears.

Other books by Al Pickett

- *Team of the Century: The Greatest High School Football Team in Texas*
- *The Greatest Texas Sports Stories You've Never Heard*
- *Wishbone Wisdom: Emory Bellard Texas Football Visionary*
- *Brother's Keeper: The Story of Abilene High's 2009 State Championship*
- *Mighty, Mighty Matadors: Estacado High School, Integration and Championship Season*

www.ingramcontent.com/pod-product-compliance
Lightning Source LLC
Chambersburg PA
CBHW011214120626
46545CB00008B/2989

* 9 7 9 8 9 9 9 8 8 6 5 5 1 0 *